BAD NEWS

Bad News
The Wapping Dispute

by
John Lang & Graham Dodkins

Foreword by
Tony Benn

SPOKESMAN

For Cathy and Madonna, who never once faltered.

First published in 2011 by
Spokesman
Russell House, Bulwell Lane
Nottingham NG6 0BT
England
Phone 0115 9708381   Fax 0115 9420433
e-mail elfeuro@compuserve.com

ISBN 978 085124 796 0

A CIP Catalogue is available from the British Library.

Cover design by Kavita Graphics

Printed by the Russell Press Ltd., (www.russellpress.com)

CONTENTS

Acknowledgements

We would like to thank the following.

Libby Hall, for allowing us to use her late husband's illustrations. During the dispute Tony, who was sacked from his job as a graphic artist at News Group Newspapers, created 'Strike Graphics' to produce posters, badges, t-shirts and mugs to promote the strike and raise funds. Tony died in 2008, but his work lives on in numerous publications produced by the Labour Movement.

Linda Melvern, for allowing us to use the research which exposed the clandestine events taking place behind the scenes prior to the dispute.

Ann Jackson, for donating the newspaper cuttings which were an invaluable aid to our research.

Nina Allsopp, for converting the original type-written manuscript into a state-of-the-art electronic version.

Those who created the stickers and leaflets in support of the strike, which are reproduced throughout the book.

The clerical strikers, whose testimonies give such honesty to the book, and those who transcribed the audio tapes.

Finally, and most importantly, *all the strikers* who remained loyal to the strike for 13 long months.

John Lang & Graham Dodkins

Abbreviations

AAD	Advertising Accounts Department
ACAS	Advisory, Conciliation and Arbitration Service
AUEW	Amalgamated Union of Engineering Workers
CCG	Communist Campaign Group
EETPU	Electrical, Electronic, Telecommunications and Plumbing Union
FOC	Father of the Chapel
GLC	Greater London Council
IPC	International Publishing Corporation
LCDTU	Liaison Committee for the Defence of Trade Unions
LDC	London District Council (SOGAT)
L&GPSG	Lesbian and Gay Print Workers Support Group
LMB	London Machine Branch (SOGAT)
LPCA	London Press Clerks' Association
MGN	Mirror Group Newspapers
MOC	Mother of the Chapel
NALGO	National Association of Local Government Officers
NATSOPA	National Society of Operative Printers and Assistants
NCCL	National Council for Civil Liberties
NEC	National Executive Committee (SOGAT)
NGA	National Graphical Association
NGN	News Group Newspapers
NUC	National Union of Clerks
NUJ	National Union of Journalists
RIRMA	Revisers, Ink Rollers and Manufacturers' Assistants
SOGAT	Society of Graphical and Allied Trades
TGWU	Transport and General Workers' Union
TNL	Times Newspapers Ltd
TNT	Thomas Nationwide Transport
TUC	Trades Union Congress

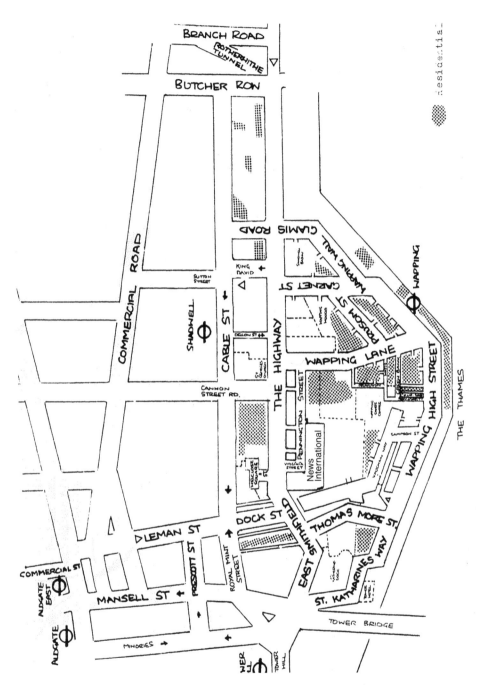

Map of the area around the Wapping plant

Foreword
Tony Benn

This book about the Wapping dispute published 25 years after it took place is timely and relevant because it reminds us of a very significant event in recent labour history.

Before the advent of computer technology printers worked with hot metal to set up the type and this practice was followed by newspapers including *The Times*, *Sunday Times*, *News of the World* and *The Sun*.

Inevitably, this new technology destroyed the work of highly skilled workers upon whom the newspapers had depended, but who were now seen as redundant and, in the drive for increased profits, the Murdoch press dismissed them.

The Thatcher Government took up the case for Murdoch and huge demonstrations were held at Wapping in which the full power of the state was mobilized against the printers with the Metropolitan Police being called in to destroy these demonstrations.

Like many people I went regularly to take part in these demonstrations in support of the printers, and saw the police in action in a way that was violent and unjustified.

Following so soon after the great Miners' Strike, this was another vivid example of the determination of the Thatcher Government to destroy the trade union movement, and was seen as such by those who had an opportunity to see what was going on.

In this sense this was also a major political event because the Thatcher Government was engaged in a campaign to undermine the Labour Party by the destruction of trade unions, the attacks on local government and the privatization of public assets.

Amongst those who went on strike and were then sacked were 600 clerical workers, half of whom were women. This book tells the story of their struggle against Murdoch and the state.

What comes out in this book is the courage and determination of those who fought for their jobs and their rights against a government that was bitterly hostile to both. But more important than that, this book is being brought out at a time of renewed attacks which has also produced a strong and broad campaign by those who would suffer if the cuts went through. It is relevant to those in current struggle and will, I am sure, give them encouragement. This is a book that should be very widely read.

1
Hokey Cokey

Joyce: *I couldn't do picket duties during the day because of the kids, so Wapping was my place. I was there an awful lot on Saturday nights until I got nicked in the June. It was my own silly fault: it was two o'clock in the morning and we were doing the Hokey Cokey along The Highway towards Tower Hill – just as a bunch of plods were coming down the other way. The next minute I'm up front: I volunteered (Sergeant Major's daughter). I should have known better and the police came swooping around in a horse-shoe shape. On every other occasion I can remember, a senior officer made a formal request through a loud hailer to clear The Highway, but it didn't happen that night. They swooped around us and I remember a girl shouting, 'Let me out, let me out'. But it was like a tube, if you'd wanted to bottle out you couldn't have done it, there was no way out. But I didn't want to get out, did I? Then this copper got hold of the back of my hair, he yanked my head back and I was kicking, but I had those Chinese slippers on with soft bottoms, so I didn't hurt him. Then Police Constable K went wallop under my chin and it was an instant reaction. I never thought about them being police or anything and I said, 'Don't you do that to me', and I tried to do it back to him, just managing to reach him with my fingers. He said I punched him on the chin – I wish I had! The next thing I know I'm getting nicked! Police Constable G, one of K's mates, came up to help him and they grabbed me. 'Right, you're nicked'. I flipped then. 'Help me, help me'. It was actually happening to me. They grabbed my right arm and they were trying to keep hold of my left arm and I lost my watch and my shoes came off because my feet were lifted off the ground. They pulled me out and dragged me down the road and G, wonderful chap that he was, had my arm up my back and I was screaming because he was really hurting my arm. I'm told that this hold with your arm up your back, bending your elbow the wrong way, they know exactly how far to go without breaking your arm. What they did was rupture the ligaments across the elbow.*

They dragged me down Virginia Street and I said, 'for Christ's sake let go of my arm, you're breaking it. Two of you have nicked me, I'm not going anywhere'. And one of them said, 'If I wanted to fucking break your arm I could break it'. There was a big pile of horse shit in the road and he said, 'You're lucky we don't make you walk in that'. He was a real nasty. I'm screaming out

11

my name and my phone number and a couple of the old boys who were picketing the gate came over and said, 'Are you all right love. Leave off mate, you're hurting her'.

They bundled me into a jeep with some other people and I was saying, 'My kids are indoors'. And this Sergeant said, 'Well what are you doing here then if you've got kids? Who's looking after them while you're down here?' and I said, 'Who's looking after yours? Telling me, 'cause I'm a mother, I shouldn't be on the picket line. You're a policeman, you shouldn't be beating people up'.

They took us round the back doubles in this Land Rover thing, to the 'meat-wagon' which was somewhere behind Thomas More Street. We were shoved into the back. When we got to Southwark nick it was surreal. I've never thought of it this way before, but it was just like when I had my son Sean. I was full of drugs then and I didn't know what the hell was going on. They took him away afterwards and kept him in a special baby care unit and when I woke up the next day I didn't have the baby near me. I got up and I remember thinking, 'I'd better go and see my child, I had a baby yesterday'. It was like it happened to somebody else and it was the same feeling when I was put in the nick.

I'd said to G, when he'd done my arm in, 'What's your number. I'm going to have you'. And he told me proudly, as a boast. When we got to the police station in all the turmoil, I'd got this number in my head but I kept thinking, 'No, that isn't right, I must have it wrong'. But I was sitting next to this copper, waiting to go to the charge desk, and I turned to him and asked if I'd got the number right. He'd written it on the palm of his hand and told me I had it right. Then he went into the Desk Sergeant and alleged that I'd punched him on the chin. It was K, the arresting officer.

I put down 'Ms' on the form and they all thought it was hysterical. They told me what I was charged with and I said, 'You've got to be joking. Never mind that, what about what they've done to my arm'. I was aware of a burning feeling, it was really sore and I said, 'I want to see a police doctor because I've been assaulted. I may well make a formal complaint'. He was very correct, the Sergeant.

I was searched by a policewoman and she was quite apologetic. They sat me in a cell and eventually the doctor came. I went to see him and the policewoman came in with me. She had to help me take my jacket off and when I lifted my arm I screamed with the pain. When I looked at it my elbow was more than twice its normal size. I cried then and I looked at the policewoman and said, 'And you wonder why we feel like we do. Look at me, look at the size of me. Two big bastards did that. In my bloody bare feet and all'. I was in tears and she looked ashamed and her eyes went down and I screamed when they took my shirt off. And the surgeon just looked at it and he said to me, 'I don't think anything's broken but I would advise, when you're released, you get it checked at your local hospital. Get an x-ray'. And then I got banged up again.

They'd taken a polaroid when I went in, ostensibly so they wouldn't confuse me with anybody else, but as I was the only woman arrested I find that a little astonishing. Then I had to go and get my fingerprints taken. The same woman did my prints, while a wise-guy in the corner was asking me questions. 'And what did you do to this officer <u>Ms</u>?' He thought this was funny and I said to the policewoman, 'I see chauvinism is alive and kicking in this nick', and she said, 'Its rampant throughout the entire Metropolitan Police Force'. I don't expect that lady can still be in the force. She seemed very disillusioned with them. She was really good to me, she said, 'If this hurts ...' She had to take a palm print and she couldn't do it properly on one hand because I couldn't turn my arm and she said, 'Don't worry, we'll just do what we can. I don't want to hurt you'.

Then this big-wig came down from Leman Street and he had a hard-nut with him. He was a uniformed Inspector and the other one was in plain clothes. He was very correct and polite. He said, 'I understand you have a complaint'. 'Would you like to tell me about it'. I was equally correct. 'I appreciate you coming over at this time in the morning, but I don't wish to make a statement or a formal complaint at this moment and you will also appreciate that it is four o'clock in the morning and I'm very tired and distressed and in pain, and very worried about getting home to my children. I'd like to take specialist advice before I formulate a complaint, but I appreciate you coming over'.

I came out and there was Karen and Chrissie (two fellow strikers) waiting for me. I didn't know they had waited. They brought me all the way home. I didn't sleep at all and later in the morning I spoke to John, who gave me the best advice a chapel official could give. 'Don't use SOGAT solicitors, you'll end up in Holloway'.

The magistrate was brilliant; I could have given him a big kiss. He let me tell the whole story when he could have dismissed it all as totally irrelevant. I told him the truth and he actually made, in so many words, a recommendation that I sue. My solicitor said we should pursue the complaint, but he moved to another firm and had a lot on his plate and it got left. I was dubious whether the branch was going to underwrite it and – in the end – I just thought that I couldn't go through it all again and I let it go. I was sorry I did but, at the end of the day, it was never going to hurt the bugger who hurt me. If I'd got compensation, the money wouldn't have come out of his pocket and he wouldn't have got a blemish on his record. People have done far worse without being demoted or even having a black mark on their record. It beats any kind of closed shop that we were supposed to have. They get away with it. The fact that I got *off was my vindication. It was really hard, but I put appeals out and found witnesses. Someone's mum – it was the first time she had been to Wapping – saw it happen. She said she'd seen several people arrested that night, but I was the only woman and the only one that was man-handled. And all the girls and blokes down at the gate turned up in court. It was lovely and I didn't know them from Adam. But nobody was called because the magistrate said it was unnecessary.*

G didn't turn up, he was at the Crown Court that day and my heart sank when I saw K. He was a baby-faced blonde and I thought, 'Shit, magistrates believe what coppers tell them. One look at him and I've no chance'. But they sent some hard-faced, thick-set guy to make their apologies for G and he was beaming all over his face. Afterwards, in the street outside, one of the women shouted at him, 'There you go, the truth will out. You can't always win'. And then we all went to the pub.

2

Rupert Murdoch's British Empire

Rupert Murdoch first became the owner of a newspaper when, following the death of his father in October 1952, he inherited *The Adelaide News*. He was 22 and in his final year of study at Oxford University. His first experience of Fleet Street followed graduation, when he did a stint as a sub editor at *The Daily Express*.

On arrival back in Australia, he soon began to expand his business, initially buying small newspapers across the country and, in 1957, entered the fledgling medium of television when his Southern Television Corporation was granted a licence to broadcast a new channel in Adelaide. He continued to build his company, News Limited, and in 1964 created *The Australian*, the first national newspaper in Australia.

Biographies of Murdoch show that he was not afraid to take risks to get what he wanted and that he could be ruthless. In his autobiography *Good Times, Bad Times* Harold Evans, former editor of *The Sunday Times* and *The Times,* quotes a description of Murdoch given him by John Barry, a journalist on *The Sunday Times*. Barry had been in negotiations with Murdoch on behalf of the National Union of Journalists (NUJ) and, wafting his hand like a shark's tail, said 'the man's charm is lethal. One minute he's swimming along with a smile, then snap! There's blood in the water. Your head's gone'.

By the late 1960s Murdoch had established himself as a major power within the newspaper industry in Australia and was now looking to expand overseas. The opportunity to acquire a British national newspaper arrived in 1968 when a disgruntled member of the Carr family, owners of *The News of the World*, wanted to sell his shares at a price the chairman, Sir William Carr, could not afford. With 25% of the shares up for sale Robert Maxwell, who was at that time a Labour MP, emerged as the only serious bidder. The Carrs were very much part of the British establishment and the thought of a socialist MP and foreigner (Maxwell was born in Slovakia) taking a major stake in their newspaper was abhorrent to them. The paper even printed an editorial calling Maxwell by his real name, Jan

Ludwig Hoch, and stating that *The News of the World* was 'a British newspaper, run by British people. Let's keep it that way'.

Despite this nationalistic fervour and with no other bidders coming forward, Murdoch was able to convince the Carrs to do a deal in which News Limited would get 40% of the voting shares in return for assets which would guarantee income of over £1 million a year. In addition, Murdoch would become Managing Director. In return, Murdoch agreed that he would not increase his stake above 40% and that Sir William Carr would stay as Chairman. In January 1969, after considerable muck slinging between Murdoch and Maxwell, the shareholders agreed the Murdoch proposals.

Within a short period of time Murdoch had reneged on the deal that had persuaded the Carrs to back him. After just a few weeks he had increased his shareholding to nearly 50% and by June had convinced the ailing Sir William Carr to stand down. At the board meeting that followed Murdoch was elected Chairman.

With *The News of the World* presses in Bouverie Street being used only once a week, Murdoch was keen to add a daily newspaper to his stable. By November 1969 he had purchased *The Sun* (which, like *The News of the World*, was a broadsheet) from the International Publishing Corporation. IPC, which at that time also published *The Daily Mirror*, had bought *The Daily Herald* in 1961 and re-launched it as *The Sun* in 1964. IPC's market research indicated that the new and better educated working class wanted a more sophisticated newspaper than the traditional tabloids. However, by 1969, *The Sun's* circulation had fallen from 1.5 million to 850,000 and was losing money. IPC wanted to either close or off-load the paper. They could not merge it with *The Daily Mirror*, because they had promised not to when they bought *The Daily Herald*, and the merger would have been referred to the Monopolies and Mergers Commission.

Once again Robert Maxwell was the only other serious bidder. Murdoch's bid was successful, in part, because it was supported by the print unions, who opposed Maxwell's proposal for several hundred job losses if he gained ownership. Murdoch bought the newspaper at a bargain price, paying an initial £50,000, with installments of £2,500 a week up to a minimum of £250,000 and a maximum of £500,000 if the paper made a continual profit. Murdoch printed *The Sun* using the same presses as *The News of the World* at Bouverie Street. In November 1969, the first tabloid edition appeared and within 12 months its circulation had doubled, with many of the new readers having come from *The Daily Mirror*.

It was another decade before Murdoch increased his ownership of national newspapers in Britain. In October 1980, Thomson British Holdings, the British subsidiary of the Canadian company, International Thomson Organization, announced that it proposed to sell Times Newspapers Ltd (TNL), which published *The Times* (with its three supplements) and *The Sunday Times*. Thomson's had purchased *The Sunday Times* in 1959, at which time it was unconnected with *The Times*, which they subsequently bought in 1967. In 1975, *The Times* moved into a new building next to *The Sunday Times* in Grays Inn Road and the papers began to be printed from the same presses.

The decision to sell followed the closure of the papers between November 1978 and November 1979. This had come about when Thomson's tried to introduce new working conditions, including direct inputting, a computerized system which would allow journalists and advertising copytakers (clerical members) to type copy straight onto the system. This new technology meant that the typesetters, who were members of the National Graphical Association (NGA), would be by-passed. The NGA saw the introduction of this technology as a direct threat to their members' jobs and insisted that any items typed by non NGA members be retyped by their members.

After lengthy negotiations and a number of stoppages, Thomson's told the print unions that unless they agreed to uninterrupted production and the establishment of the new technology, the papers would be shut down. The journalists agreed a new deal on their working conditions just hours before the deadline management had set for all unions to reach a settlement. No agreement was forthcoming with the other unions and the papers were closed.

After 12 months, during which time journalists and management continued to be paid and no agreement was reached, the papers re-opened. It was estimated that the dispute cost Thomson's £40 million. Following a further dispute in August 1980 (this time with the journalists who wanted a large pay rise) and with pre-tax losses for the year expected to be £15 million, Thomson's decided to sell.

Other options had been considered by the Thomson Board, including immediate closure of both papers and the dismissal of the majority of the workforce for misconduct, which would have relieved the company of their obligation to make redundancy payments estimated to be around £36 million.

The papers were put up for sale on 22nd October 1980 and

Thomson's set the deadline for bids at 31ˢᵗ December. In an effort to pressurize the unions, a further deadline of early March 1981 was set for negotiations with the successful bidder to be concluded. If this was not achieved, both newspapers would be closed, leaving Thomson's with the responsibility for the aforementioned £36 million redundancy payments. In setting these conditions, the company had put pressure on itself to ensure that the sale went ahead.

As well as Murdoch's News International, there were several serious bidders including Associated Newspapers, Lonrho and Atlantic Richfield (owners of *The Observer*). In addition, the editors of the papers, William Rees-Mogg of *The Times* and Harold Evans of *The Sunday Times* both tried, but failed, to form separate consortiums to buy their own individual publication. Rupert Murdoch's initial bid was put on the table one day before the 31ˢᵗ December deadline. He offered £1 million and demanded that *The Sunday Times* building be thrown in free. He also wanted Thomson to bear the £1 million plus cost of management redundancies. Murdoch described the bid as '… getting my foot in the door'.

As part of the agreement of Thomson's purchase of *The Times* in 1967, four independent national directors had been appointed whose role included the protection of editorial content from interference by the proprietor. These national directors, along with the two editors and Denis Hamilton, the Editor in Chief of both newspapers, formed the vetting committee for the potential bidders. In his autobiography, Harold Evans describes the committee's meeting with Murdoch and how he had agreed to all that they had asked of him. This had included non-interference by the proprietor in the 'selection and balance of the news', and that the national directors would approve the appointment of editors. Murdoch also reluctantly agreed that Times Newspapers Limited would remain a separate company from News International and, by inference, *The Sun* and *The News of the World*.

The deal eventually struck was a bargain for Murdoch: News International paid £12 million in cash for the two newspapers and the supplements. They did not have to pay back any of the £92 million which Thomson's had pumped into TNL over the previous 14 years and Thomson's had to pay £250,000 towards redundancy payments for senior managers. Murdoch's offer was not the best that Thomson's received: Associated Newspapers had offered £25 million for the profitable *Sunday Times* alone and £20 million if they had to take the loss-making *Times,* whilst insisting that they could close *The Times* if they chose. Thomson's, who as part of any deal, were going to keep a stake in TNL for the following 10 years, were adamant that both papers must be purchased as going concerns and the unions, who faced large job losses if *The Times* was closed, supported this position.

To put the sum that Murdoch paid into perspective, it was estimated that the value of the freehold of *The Sunday Times* building, together with assets such as vehicles and machinery, came to around £26 million.

Despite the fact that the deal left Murdoch owning a third of the national newspapers in Britain, John Biffen, Secretary of State for Trade in Margaret Thatcher's Conservative Government, announced that the bid would not be referred to the Monopolies and Mergers Commission on the grounds that neither paper was economic. Many in the Labour Movement saw this as a reward to Murdoch for his political support of the Tories. Despite this, the leaders of the main print unions, The National Society of Operative Printers and Assistants (NATSOPA), the Society of Graphic and Allied Tades (SOGAT) and the NGA wrote to the Labour Party leader, Michael Foot, asking him not to press for an enquiry, stating that the papers would be 'killed off'. Biffen's decision was challenged by some MPs in Parliament and by *The Sunday Times* NUJ chapel*, who knew, having seen the financial prospectus drawn up by the accountants at the time of the sale, that *The Sunday Times* could be profitable and decided to fight the decision in court.

The journalists never got to court, however. Thirty-six hours before the hearing was due, Murdoch offered them a deal: in exchange for halting the legal action, he offered further guarantees on editorial independence, plus the appointment of two working journalists to the newspapers' board. The NUJ argued amongst themselves but, eventually, agreed to the offer.

Three weeks were left for negotiations to take place with the trade union chapels representing 4,000 full and part-time TNL employees. Murdoch demanded major staffing cuts; a strict procedure for avoiding unofficial disputes, which included built-in cash penalties;

---

*Each group of workers belonged to their own individual workplace trade union known as a Chapel. The earliest reference to this type of organisation is in Joseph Moxon's *Mechanick Exercises* (1863). Moxon states that: 'Every Printing House, by custom of time out of mind, is called a Chapel and all the workmen that belong to it are members of the Chapel'.

and a one year wage freeze. But he made concessions: the cash penalties were lifted, the wage freeze would last only three months and the redundancies would be voluntary. In return, *The Times* supplements would be contracted out, 563 permanent jobs (including 130 out of 800 clerical positions) and over 100 one-night shifts would go over the following six months. New technology would be brought in, but without editorial or advertising direct entry, one of the issues that had led to the year-long shut down.

Within a year Murdoch was seeking further redundancies and the clerical chapels were his main target. In January 1982, the company gave six months notice of the termination of the existing agreements between itself and the unions. However, the company immediately started sending out redundancy notices and letters to the remainder asking them to consider taking voluntary redundancy. Murdoch was demanding 600 redundancies from the two papers, of which 250 were clerical posts, stating that if he did not get the numbers he required he would close both of the papers. As with the original takeover, negotiations went to the brink, but eventually agreements were reached and the clerical chapels lost 200 posts through the process of voluntary redundancy.

At the same time as these redundancy negotiations were taking place, it was discovered that Murdoch had unlawfully transferred the two newspaper titles from the ownership of TNL to News International. The transfer meant that if he put TNL into liquidation, the titles would not be among the assets available to the receiver and consequently would prevent a rival publisher from buying the papers. Murdoch had carried out the transfer without the knowledge of the national directors and, consequently had broken one of the pledges that he had given to the Government which allowed him to avoid referral to the Monopolies Commission. Following much criticism, including from *The Times,* and rejection of the move by the national directors, the transfer was reversed.

3
Unions Under Attack
Shah – Warrington – NGA

On 3rd May 1979 the Conservative Party, led by Margaret Thatcher, won the general election. One of their main campaign themes was to reduce, what they perceived to be, the power of the trade unions. This followed a series of mainly public sector strikes in the winter of 1978/79 which *The Sun*, plagiarizing Shakespeare, dubbed 'The Winter of Discontent'. The paper was prominent in its support of the Tories and, in the lead up to the election, printed a series of articles by disillusioned former Labour Party Ministers. On election day, its front page headline read 'VOTE TORY THIS TIME'. In the 1980 New Year's Honours list Larry Lamb, the paper's editor, duly received a knighthood for services to journalism

The legislative attack on the unions started with the 1980 Employment Act, which eroded the closed shop,* restricted lawful picketing to the workplace of those in dispute and limited the maximum number of people allowed on a picket line to six. It also made solidarity (or secondary) action by unions not involved in the dispute illegal. This was followed by the 1982 Employment Act limiting the definition of a 'trade dispute' which, when coupled with the 1980 Act, outlawed practically all forms of solidarity action, including by members of the same union. The 1982 Act also placed further restrictions on the closed shop and empowered employers to fire striking workers, without facing unfair dismissal claims, if they sacked all workers involved in the strike at a particular workplace on a particular day. In addition it made trade unions legally liable to pay disabling damages resulting from strikes. Fines of up to £250,000 could be imposed and if these were not paid, the union's entire funds could be sequestrated.**

In response to the 1982 Act, a Trade Union Congress (TUC) Special Conference was held in April 1982 and trade union leaders

---

*A workplace where all employees were required to be union members as a precondition to employment.
**Confiscated and held by a third party.

voted to support an eight-point plan to oppose the Act. A campaign pack entitled *Fight Tebbit's Law* (the act had been introduced by the then Secretary of State Norman Tebbit), was issued and a travelling exhibition toured trade union conferences. Trade union leaders voted overwhelmingly at the TUC Conference on 7th September 1982 for militant resistance, including industrial action.

The then TUC General Secretary, Len Murray, said of the campaign: we cannot be sure that we can deliver ... Government propaganda has even found credence among many of our members who value what their own unions do for them but are, paradoxically and illogically, at best apathetic and, at worst, sympathetic to the Government's purpose. We have a major job alerting trade unionists themselves to the real nature of the proposals. Bill Keys, General Secretary of SOGAT, stated: 'I will say publicly anywhere, if it is a bad law that doesn't nurture good, that doesn't look after the interests of ordinary people in this nation, I will oppose the law and I will influence other people to oppose the law ... if that means breaking the law I will do it.'

It would not be long before the trade union movement came into direct conflict with these laws.

In 1983, Eddie Shah became a household name when a local dispute with the NGA sprang to national prominence. Shah owned his own typesetting company, Fineward, based in Stockport. His newspapers were of the free-sheet variety, containing little news coverage and depending on advertising revenue. There was a closed-shop agreement with the NGA. Problems began when Shah announced that he intended to start a newspaper in Bury, with wages some £40 a week less than employees earned at Stockport. It was also discovered that he had installed computerized typesetting equipment, which secretaries were being trained to use.

Having then purchased a second-hand printing press for installation at Winwick Quay, Warrington, he moved to recruit non-union staff both here and at Bury. The NGA attempted to prevent this and, eventually, a compromise was reached whereby the NGA could enter both plants and invite staff to join the union. The employees had been hand-picked by the company and it was hardly surprising when they unanimously rejected the invitation. The NGA then instructed its eight members at Stockport to withdraw their labour. Two refused, but the remaining six walked out on 4th July. Shah sacked them three weeks later. The situation remained relatively low key for the next few months, with negotiations continuing, but Shah refused to reinstate the six sacked workers.

In mid-November, picketing organized by the NGA began outside the Warrington plant. This brought the union into direct conflict with the 1980 and 1982 Employment Acts regarding secondary action and Shah sought and obtained an injunction against the union. The ruling was ignored and picketing continued. At this stage, there were about 500 people involved and the police had little difficulty in securing the exit of the newspaper vans. A fine of £50,000 for contempt of court was imposed on the NGA and this came with a warning that the union's assets could be sequestrated. They refused to pay the fine and it was made clear that action would be expected from their Fleet Street members if sequestration took place. The local dispute was becoming a national trade union issue.

The fine remained unpaid and the picket grew larger. On 25th November, the union was fined another £100,000 for contempt and the seizure of their assets, believed to be around £11 million, was ordered. An appeal court judge overturned that ruling, but ordered the sequestration of a further £175,000 pending a full appeal hearing. The NGA members in Fleet Street walked out and all national newspaper production stopped for the next two days. The proprietors threatened injunctions against the NGA and demanded assurances that there would be no more Fleet Street stoppages in support of the Warrington dispute. The union refused to give any such assurances and the unity of the proprietors quickly disintegrated as they made individual deals for a return to work.

With secondary picketing continuing, the original sequestration order against the NGA was re-imposed and the Fleet Street proprietors were also granted an injunction forbidding any further stoppages by the NGA.

On the night of 29th November, 5,000 pickets gathered outside the Warrington plant – many having travelled from Fleet Street – and witnessed, for the first time, scenes that were to become commonplace during the Miners' and Wapping disputes.

There were around 1,000 police present and snatch squads were used to remove demonstrators at the front of the crowd. The NGA back-up van was seized by the police and at around 3am, the Tactical Aid Group (a northern Special Patrol Group) attacked the crowd without warning. They were wearing helmets and visors and carrying 'nightsticks' and, to ensure their actions were not recorded, television arc lights were ordered to be turned off. The plant, along with other industrial units, was in the middle of a large field and many demonstrators were chased by police Land Rovers with their headlights on full-beam. At around 4am, the first newspapers left the plant with little resistance and a larger picket, promised for the following night, never materialized.

Clerical members from the TNL Chapel who were present that night reported these events to their chapel meeting a couple of weeks later, but the reaction indicated that lots of people either did not believe, or did not want to believe, the account of police actions.

Further demonstrations and picketing took place and the NGA turned to the TUC for assistance. The Employment Policy and Organization Committee voted by nine to seven to 'take a sympathetic and supportive view', but Len Murray spoke out on TV against the decision and then called an emergency General Council meeting at which it was reversed.

The TUC's first major confrontation with the anti-union laws had been met with a resounding back down and the NGA were left high and dry, with no alternative but to call off the strike.

The following year saw the introduction of the 1984 Trade Union Act, which made it illegal to strike without a secret ballot and ordered unions to instruct their members that they would be breaking their contract of employment if they voted in favour of strike action. The anti-union legislation was to play a major role in the Wapping dispute.

As for Shah, in March 1986 he launched *Today*, a national daily newspaper which was the first to use colour printing. He made a single union agreement with Eric Hammond, General Secretary of the Electrical, Electronic, Telecommunications and Plumbing Union (EETPU) who, in return for the single union status, agreed that there would be no closed shop or demarcation lines between union and non-union staff. Hammond, too, would be a key player at Wapping.

Within four months of its launch Shah, who had apparently overstretched himself financially, had sold *Today* to Lonrho, which, since its unsuccessful bid for TNL, had become owners of *The Observer*.

4

The Wapping Plant

Six months prior to the start of the dispute, few clerical workers at Gray's Inn Road had heard of the Wapping plant and even during the lead up to the strike, an 'out of sight, out of mind' mentality prevailed. It was just the place where News Group Newspapers (NGN), *The Sun* and *The News of the World*, were to be printed. The clerical members at News Group were not part of the planned move from Bouverie Street, so it was not until the strike loomed that the clericals became involved at all.

The 13 acre site at Wapping in East London, less than half a mile east of Tower Bridge, was purchased by Murdoch in 1978 and building work commenced in 1980. The old, worn out printing presses at Bouverie Street, constantly running at very high speeds in a cramped Machine Room, were at the end of their tether and health and safety conditions were appalling, with workers exposed to ink spray, paper dust, excessive heat and noise and the danger of metal plates shattering during a print run.

But it wasn't the welfare of the workers that was uppermost in Murdoch's mind when Wapping was initiated. *The Sun* alone earned him an estimated £26 million per year, but the money was desperately needed to finance other ventures: News Corporation, the parent company of News International, had borrowed heavily in 1985 to purchase six television stations from Metromedia, America's largest independent television network, and the 50% of Twentieth Century Fox Film Corporation which it did not already own, for a combined cost of around $2 billion. (Murdoch became a United States citizen to enable him to meet the legal requirements which would allow him ownership of the television stations he purchased from Metromedia.) With greater printing capacity for *The Sun* and *The News of the World*, even more profits could be made and, despite stating that industrial relations problems were costing him money, he knew that the eventual breakdown of the machinery was a much more immediate threat.

Negotiations with the News Group Newspapers' chapels for the move to the new plant began in May 1983. Talks broke down in March '84, reopened in September of that year and, in January 1985, *The News of the World* machine chapel reached agreement with News Group for the move. They were the only chapel to achieve a settlement, which included the loss of 90 of their 475 jobs. Within a few weeks, negotiations with other chapels were suspended by the company and, in March 1985, it was announced that a completely new newspaper would be printed at Wapping. *The Post* was going to be Britain's first 24 hour paper, with morning editions being distributed nationally and afternoon and evening editions in London only. But the national aspirations of the new paper were later dropped and it became known as the *London Post*.

There was little or no reaction to these proposals from the clerical workforce, who still viewed Wapping from afar as just a printing facility. *The Times* was celebrating its bi-centenary and staff were presented with commemorative mugs, bottles of specially labelled champagne and a book entitled *The Times Past, Present and Future*. The future of the paper was contemplated in an idealistic article by the editor Charles Douglas-Home, which gave no clue to the carnage to come:

> 'We are now at the start of a period of expansion which I hope will be one of the most distinctive in our history', he wrote. 'The electronic age must be exploited by us to produce a better newspaper ... Electronic techniques will enable journalists to work faster and to call on more sources of information and research. They should also enable the paper to be produced at lower cost, so that we might even be able to reduce its price.'

The London Post was no more than a front, a tactic designed to divert attention from News International's secret preparations for printing its four national newspapers at Wapping without the print unions.

As early as February 1985, Murdoch had gathered around him a team to carry out his plan. Some members were well known at Bouverie Street and Gray's Inn Road: Bruce Matthews was Managing Director of News International; Charles Wilson was to become editor of *The Times* following the death of Charles Douglas-Home, and Bill Gillespie was managing director of Times Newspapers Limited.

Murdoch summoned his key executives to New York and ordered them to plan secretly for the move, while orders for £10 million worth of equipment were placed with the American computer company Atex. This equipment was secretly imported into Britain and set up and tested in a warehouse at an old industrial site in Woolwich, South-

East London, by American computer experts. A security firm was engaged to guard the warehouse day and night.

In April 1985, News International executive John Keating, along with Christopher Pole-Carew, who was responsible for security at Wapping, and Tom Rice, an official of the EETPU responsible for national newspapers, toured America inspecting computerized typesetting equipment. It was at this stage that the EETPU began secretly planning with the company to work out the staffing levels needed to operate the printing equipment.

Security was stepped up at Wapping in June. Entrance to the plant could only be gained with a special pass and closed circuit TV and electronically controlled gates were installed. The high steel fences erected earlier in the year were reinforced with razor wire.

During the same month, a £7 million order for nearly 1,000 vehicles was placed with the British subsidiary of Thomas Nationwide Transport (TNT), an Australian firm which Murdoch jointly owned with Ansett, Australia's second largest airline company. A five-year distribution contract, worth £1 million a week, was placed with the company, thereby bypassing the railways and the wholesale distribution companies where SOGAT had 100% union membership. It was a vital part of Murdoch's plan.

Prior to the company withdrawing from negotiations, union representatives had been allowed access to the Wapping plant. In July 1983, following a request from his chapel, a Deputy Father of the Chapel* (FOC) from the Amalgamated Union of Engineering Workers (AUEW) at News Group had been given permission to enter the building by the senior management of News International and, following a similar request in October 1983, a health and safety representative from the SOGAT Revisers, Ink Rollers and Manufacturers' Assistants (RIRMA) Branch** at News Group was also given access. They were working on behalf of their chapels to carry out an assessment of the equipment at the plant in order to evaluate the staffing numbers they would require. Despite being from different unions, they worked together and in June 1984 produced a comprehensive 102 page technical report. In general, the report was positive about the working conditions and the future for their members at Wapping.

---

* A Father of the Chapel is a senior shop steward.
**Branches were the organizations representing different chapels at various workplaces.

The AUEW requested that more of their engineering staff be given access to see the machinery and, during the course of November 1984, 92 of their chapel members were shown around Wapping. Then, on the 5ᵗʰ December, the management suddenly instructed that no more AUEW members were to be allowed on the site. Within a few weeks, security had been increased at the plant and, by March 1985, management had suspended talks with all the News Group chapels and had announced its proposals for printing *The Post* at Wapping.

The union reps, however, had made a number of contacts with 'insiders' during their time at Wapping and information continued to be leaked to them, including the fact that two floors in the building had been sealed off. They were then informed of plans to convert some of the presses from tabloid to broadsheet (the format of *The Times* and *Sunday Times*) and immediately contacted the office of Brenda Dean, General Secretary of SOGAT, from which they received no response. They also began to receive staffing details, which included a 19-page list of companies contracted to work at the site and the names of over 500 employees. Following further leaks from their contacts inside the plant, they posed as prospective customers with a company which supplied polymer letterpress printing plates. This technology was not new, but they asked if they could see it tested anywhere and were told that Murdoch was testing it at Wapping, although this was supposed to be a secret.

In May 1985, the UK Press Gazette announced the appointment of Christopher Pole-Carew as 'Consultant for New Technology' at *The Post*. But Murdoch had employed him some three months earlier and, as previously stated, he had already been on a ' fact finding tour' to America, where he was looking at computerized typesetting equipment. Pole-Carew was well known for his union-busting activities: as managing director of T Bailey Forman, publishers of the *Nottingham Evening Post*, he had been instrumental in sacking 300 printers in a 1973 dispute over new technology and 28 journalists during a pay dispute in 1978. He had been responsible for a security system at the Nottingham paper which included identity cards and closed-circuit TV. Security was to be his role at Wapping.

Despite providing the leaked information from within Wapping, the whistle blowers complained, 'no one paid any attention to us'. On 17ᵗʰ June, in what is described as 'a desperate move to warn people', RIRMA mounted an exhibition of their evidence at a London hotel but, despite the distribution of many invitations, only one full-time union official turned up. He was so concerned by what he saw, however, that he too contacted Brenda Dean and, within a week of the exhibition taking place, a meeting was set up at the Waldorf Hotel in London. Dean conducted 'an interrogation' and, thenceforth, was supplied with a continual flow of information.

Some, but by no means all, of that information was relayed to SOGAT branch and chapel officials at a meeting on 30th July at the TUC headquarters in central London:

John; *Brenda Dean revealed that she had met Murdoch earlier in the month and it appeared that she had succumbed to his divide and rule tactics, blaming the NGA for the breakdown of the Wapping negotiations. She said that unless SOGAT moved quickly, the union could be left out in the cold. Some of the Machine Branch responded to this by calling on SOGAT to do a deal at Wapping, if necessary, without the NGA.*

The following day, the National Executive announced that it was to seek talks with News Group Newspapers, suggesting there would be some movement by SOGAT over the separate issue of the production of *The Sun* in Scotland. There had been resistance by the union to a proposal that Scottish editions of the paper be printed at Kinning Park in Glasgow, because of fears that northern editions of *The News of the World*, which were printed in Manchester, would be moved there. Kinning Park was to receive little attention in London, but it was vital to Murdoch's plan and security was intensified there just as it was at Wapping.

A meeting eventually took place with the company in late August, at which Brenda Dean and Tony Dubbins, General Secretary of the NGA, were both present. After the meeting, Dean issued a press statement in which she described how she had met with Bruce Matthews and Christopher Pole-Carew and that she was 'pleased to say that they both totally denied any personnel were being recruited, were currently working in the premises, or were being trained in jobs traditionally done by SOGAT members'. The statement also said that the EETPU had been contacted and that they had confirmed that their members in Wapping were carrying out electricians' work and 'certainly were not doing any work which would normally be that of the members of SOGAT'. She also stated that Murdoch would be visiting the UK during September and that 'no agreements would be reached with any union' until this visit.

Just one week later, a dummy newspaper, very similar to *The Sun*, was printed at Wapping. In the past, this type of action by the management would have produced an immediate stoppage by the unions and there was expectation that none of Murdoch's Sunday papers, due out on the following day, would be printed. However, this time, no action was taken, with the fathers of the chapel deciding to await the outcome of the meeting that was due with Murdoch.

The News Group and Times Newspapers clerical committees met with their branch officials on 11th September to discuss the increased activity at Wapping and separate chapel meetings took place the following day. It was apparent that many people on the committees and many chapel members were unaware of the seriousness of the situation, and there was much resistance to any suggestion of industrial action. The feeling, especially at Times Newspapers, was that Wapping was not their problem, that they were being drawn into a dispute they had no wish to be involved in. On the same day as the clerical chapel meetings, the London Machine Branch held a mass meeting of its News International members and voted against a proposal from its branch committee for a 24-hour strike on all four newspapers.

Further evidence of the collusion between News International and the EETPU appeared in the middle of September when the Socialist Workers Party carried a front page story in its weekly newspaper regarding recruitment that was being carried out from the union's Southampton office. In the article, the EETPU's Branch Chair for the Southampton area told how he had discovered that the office was being used as 'a recruiting centre' for employment at Wapping and that 'over 500 men have been interviewed and recruited'. The paper reported that recruits travelled to London for a second interview where one of the first questions they were asked was 'are you prepared to cross picket lines?'

The decisions not to take any action over the dummy run must have been music to Murdoch's ears, and the delaying tactics employed to gain time for Wapping to become operational continued when he met the General Secretaries of the five print unions, SOGAT, NGA, AUEW, NUJ and EETPU, on 30th September. The electricians were still involved in the talks, which indicated that the guarantees given by them that their members were only carrying out installation work at Wapping had been accepted by the other unions. Murdoch laid down the timetable he required for *The London Post* negotiations. He told the unions that they had until Christmas to reach agreement and that no negotiations would take place concerning *The Sun* or *The News of the World* until *The Post* issue was settled. The unions' acceptance of this timetable gave him the breathing space he needed and showed that they believed that *The London Post* project was a reality despite the evidence they had received.

On 1ˢᵗ November, the company presented the unions with a document containing the proposals for the terms and conditions that their members would have to work under at *The London Post*. The document, calculated to be totally unacceptable to the unions, stipulated that:

- There would be no recognition of chapels or union branches and no negotiations with them.
- There would be no 'closed shop', with employees who were members of a union being able to leave it at any time.
- Union representatives would be elected by members, but could be removed by management if they were given a written warning for any disciplinary offence.
- There was to be no union recognition at all for supervisors and managers, many of whom were Clerical Branch members.
- There would be complete flexibility of working with no demarcation lines.
- New technology could be adopted at any time, followed by job cuts.
- There would be no minimum staffing levels, with the company deciding the number of people required for any job and their starting and finishing times.
- The company would have exclusive rights to manage and would select people for jobs, classifying and re-classifying them; hiring; promoting; demoting and transferring employees as required. They would also suspend, discipline, dismiss and lay off employees as they saw fit.
- All of this was to be legally binding on the unions and their members.

The terms and conditions that had taken many years to achieve at national newspapers were being swept away overnight at *The London Post*. One had visions of the company management sitting around a table, taking it in turns to see who could come up with the most outrageous ideas to goad the unions into taking action. The proposals were met by the members as if they were some kind of joke but, as events moved forward, an element of fear crept into the workplace.

The company's proposals and timetable for an agreement by Christmas remained totally inflexible, while the unions desperately sought a negotiated settlement because of the advanced stage of readiness of the Wapping plant. The December issue of *SOGAT Journal* gave an update of negotiations and stated that, despite the company's stance, 'talks have not broken down and we are earnestly seeking a resolution'. Ironically, it was also reported that there was a disagreement with the NGA over the staffing of the machine room at *The London Post,* with the NGA claiming 100% membership. In the face of impending disaster, old habits continued to die hard. A few weeks earlier, Bill Miles, a SOGAT General Officer with responsibility for national newspapers, had been interviewed on Channel 4 News and indicated that SOGAT would be willing, if necessary, to be involved in a single union deal at Wapping.

While negotiations continued with News International, significant events were taking place elsewhere in the industry. At the beginning of November '85, Robert Maxwell announced that he required 2,000 redundancies from a staff of 6,000 at Mirror Group Newspapers (MGN).

All union members had received notice of dismissal, to take effect from 31st December, if agreement on the redundancies was not reached by the end of November. A ballot of the MGN membership, proposing strike action and negotiations with management on cost savings and job losses if the dismissal notices were withdrawn, was carried by a majority vote and, on 24th November, strike action and picketing began and the paper failed to be published. The workforce found itself in a position of strength and, faced with a continuing stoppage, Maxwell withdrew the dismissal notices.

The SOGAT national union and, in particular, Brenda Dean, heralded the success, but then proceeded to give Maxwell almost everything he had sought in the first place, including the 2,000 redundancies and the splitting up of the company, which would result in employees working for different firms. Needless to say, the workforce was demoralized and the capitulation must have given Murdoch and the other proprietors a great boost.

Back at Gray's Inn Road, at Times Newspapers, an atmosphere of uncertainty was growing, with senior and middle ranking members of staff disappearing from work for several weeks at a time. The determinedly jocular response of the workforce put these absences down to 'Wapping Cough' and it was difficult to impress upon them the gravity of a situation that threatened to transfer their jobs to a new plant operating under such noxious conditions. The general feeling was that Wapping did not have the capacity to handle all the News International titles, but the detachment of the Times Newspapers members, their belief that the problem only concerned *The Sun* and *The News of the World*, began to change with the continuing absences of managers and, by early December, rumours began to spread that *The Times* and *The Sunday Times* were going to move to the new plant.

Denise: *The Chief Librarian went sick for about five weeks and he was the only person I've ever known to have had hepatitis and put on a stone in weight! At the time it was a joke, but later it was seriously suggested that people who were off sick were actually going over to Wapping to prepare things.*

Talks between the company and the unions were deadlocked and, on 10ᵗʰ December, the national executive committee of SOGAT recommended industrial action over the dispute with News International. It also agreed to hold a mass meeting of all members, followed immediately by a ballot. The national union was obviously hoping that the threat of industrial action would shift the company's position on negotiations.

On the 16ᵗʰ December, the TNL clerical chapel held a meeting to discuss the situation. The deadlock of talks regarding *The Post*, management's proposals for the terms and conditions at Wapping and the knock-on effect that these could have, were relayed to the members. Chapel officials made it clear that the same conditions could be imposed on the workforce at TNL if the company served notice on the existing agreements. Speakers from the floor were of the clear opinion that *The London Post* was a front for other activities and that members should prepare for the worst. People were encouraged to go to Wapping to see the huge scale of the development, the fencing, the razor wire and the security cameras.

A recommendation from the chapel committee that a fighting fund be initiated with a £1 per week levy from each chapel member was carried unanimously. The most worrying aspect of the meeting was the low attendance of members from the weaker areas of the chapel, namely the telephone and display advertising sections.

Whilst preparations for industrial action were commencing at a local level, problems were mounting nationally. At the same time as Murdoch had been meeting the print unions, members of the EETPU continued to be trained to carry out the print workers' jobs at Wapping and Kinning Park. The duplicitous role of the EETPU at Wapping and the failure of the TUC to take decisive action against them, was to cause much anger and resentment amongst those who ultimately lost their jobs. SOGAT and the NGA had, by the autumn of 1985, continued to receive information regarding branches of the EETPU in Southampton and Glasgow who were recruiting staff for Wapping and Kinning Park. This recruitment was not for electrical installation work, but training to carry out print workers' jobs. By the 17th December, when SOGAT and the NGA had submitted their evidence to make a formal complaint to the TUC, the EETPU National Executive had already decided to withdraw from being part of the joint approach in the News International negotiations.

On 23rd December, because of fears that the EETPU was attempting a single union deal at Wapping, Norman Willis, General Secretary of the TUC, wrote to the five unions negotiating with News International in an attempt to ensure that no individual agreements were made with the company without the approval of the other unions concerned. But the wheels of trade union bureaucracy were turning too slowly and, by the time the complaint against the EETPU was heard, the strike had started and the scab workforce had been crossing the picket lines for nearly a week.

When the complaint was finally heard by the TUC General Council, it was decided that the EETPU had a case to answer as their activities could be 'detrimental to the interests of the trade union movement'. The Council reconvened the following week, with EEPTU General Secretary Eric Hammond and National Officer Tom Rice present to answer the allegations made against their union.

The meeting lasted late into the night and ended with a decision the strikers considered a shameful fudge. The EETPU were issued with six directives. The expectation was that one of these would instruct their members at Wapping and Kinning Park to stop carrying out work previously undertaken by print workers. Instead, they were merely told to inform their members that they were engaging in work normally done by other trade unionists. The TUC General Council, fearful of legal action by either, or both, the EETPU and News International for issuing an illegal instruction, had made a decision which one Council member described as 'pathetic'.

Eric Hammond had been elected to take over as General Secretary of the EETPU in 1982. Having carried out the role jointly with the incumbent, Frank Chapple, for over a year, he took on the post fully in 1984. Chapple had said of his successor, 'if you think I am right wing, wait until you see Eric'. It did not take him long to build up a reputation that infuriated many other trade unions as he embraced much of the Tory anti-union legislation and expressed his regard for Margaret Thatcher. In 1984, during the year-long miners' dispute, he refused to rally the support of his members in the power stations and denounced the leadership of the National Union of Mineworkers (NUM), referring to the miners as 'lions led by donkeys'.

At the General Council meeting, Hammond had insisted that the recruitment from the branches at Southampton and Glasgow had gone ahead without his knowledge and Rice had stated that 'we, the EETPU, had no contact with Pole Carew'.

In his autobiography, aptly titled *Maverick*, Hammond tells how Murdoch had approached him and asked if the electricians could set up the machinery at Wapping. He replied, 'not only that, they could operate it as well'. He recounts that there was an 'audible click as Rupert suddenly realized that here was an opportunity to end print union power once and for all'. 'He turned to me and said "Eric, I think we might be able to do a deal". The rest is history'. Despite Hammond's connivance, Murdoch refused to formally recognize the EETPU at Wapping and Kinning Park and a single union deal was never signed. Hammond states in his autobiography that Murdoch had not shown 'one spark of gratitude'.

At the end of December, Murdoch had announced that he was going ahead with *The London Post* without trade union agreement. The announcement was timed to ensure that there would be minimal immediate reaction due to the imminence of the New Year holiday.

The pace of events quickened sharply in January. An emergency meeting of the TNL clerical committee on the 7th agreed that it was essential to ensure, through the provision of adequate transportation, that members attend the mass meeting on the 13th January called by the SOGAT National Executive and that they be encouraged to vote for industrial action. On the 8th, the first joint meeting of the News Group Newspapers and TNL clerical chapel committees took place.

The TNL chapel had a reputation for organization and strength, much of it developed during the 1970s by the old *Sunday Times* chapel, prior to amalgamation with *The Times*. Many initiatives, including the nine-day fortnight achieved at *The Sunday Times*, were subsequently won by other Fleet Street clerical chapels.

18 months prior to the dispute, the amalgamated chapel had negotiated an agreement for the introduction of new technology, including a comprehensive health and safety package. The membership of around 600 was split evenly between men and women and this was reflected in the make-up of the committee and its progressive policies, which included regular cervical smear tests financed by the company.

The main discussion at the joint meeting was the mobilization for the mass meeting and working for a 'Yes' vote in the ballot for industrial action. To this end, Clerical Branch officials spoke at NGN and TNL chapel meetings on 10th January. The presence of the full-time officials on the platforms was important in emphasizing the gravity of events surrounding Wapping and the significance was not lost on the members.

If additional proof was needed that *The Sunday Times* and *The Times* were part and parcel of the plans for Wapping, it came on the following evening. *The Sunday Times* was being printed, as usual, at Gray's Inn Road when a change was made to the final edition. It carried an announcement that, the following week, the 16 page appointments supplement would be printed at, and distributed from, Wapping.

The Machine Room decided to print the final edition containing the announcement. Following meetings amongst themselves and frantic telephone calls to union officials, it was decided that Murdoch was attempting to provoke action ahead of the impending ballot. The whole question of taking industrial action without a ballot was still very fresh in people's minds following the Miners' Strike, when action had been taken without balloting the workforce, a decision which provided propaganda for the Government, divided the miners and influenced the public's perception of the strike. It soon became apparent, however, that voting before strike action was taken would not ensure protection from dismissal for the workforce.

Murdoch was actually desperate for a 'yes' vote so the workforce would go on strike and he could sack them, as suggested in a letter written by the company solicitor.

The letter from Geoffrey Richards, Senior Partner at Farrer & Co, was addressed to Bruce Matthews and copied to Murdoch. It was headed 'Strike Dismissals':

'Since the very first day I was involved in the London Post project I have advised that, if a moment came when it was necessary to dispense with the

present workforce at TNL and NGN, the cheapest way of doing so would be to dismiss employees while participating in a strike or other industrial action. A strike would be better either because it is easier to identify a striker or because only one or two people may black a particular piece of equipment and there may be a dispute as to whether others can be required to work it or not'. Richards stated ' *In that case, the person would almost certainly be repudiating his contract and could be instantly dismissed; he would not be entitled to redundancy payment; he would have no claim for unfair dismissal, providing all the workers had been fired at the same time; and the employer was under no compulsion to prove a reason for dismissal.*

Given that we are now much nearer the date of possible explosion – although I appreciate that a more 'evolutionist' approach may still (necessarily) be adopted – I thought it would be sensible, not least because some of these points came up only on Wednesday, if I reiterated the advice already given. It will be useful if the key people have the main principles of the law firmly in their heads at all times.'

Richards then gave details of how individual cases such as an employee being off sick or too frightened to take part in the strike *'could easily be mopped up'* as *'most judges have held that it is not practicable for an employer to enquire into the reasons or motives of employees for non-attendance at work'.*

Richards emphasized that any worker who was dismissed should not be re-engaged and stated that *'this may be a difficulty for us, not least because of the large numbers involved. However, in the context of the closed shops of Fleet Street, where chapel administrations hold such particular sway, it may be easier to persuade an industrial tribunal that action by a chapel is indeed action by each and every member'.*

He stressed the importance of the actual dismissal notices and their distribution. *'Dismissal notices will need to be posted over the various buildings immediately the decision is taken to dismiss. Chapel administrations must be informed immediately and letters should be sent out to each employee as quickly as possible. There may be merit in having piles of dismissal letters at exit doors, even if that involves an element of duplication'.* He continued, *'we talked about this some months ago and it may be desirable to talk about it again early in the New Year'.*

Richards continued in this calculated vane by stating *'that brings me to the last point. Both NGN and TNL operate very complicated rota systems in many departments and both publish a weekday and Sunday newspaper. Many of the Sunday employees are different to the weekday employees. The idea is to catch as many employees in the net as possible and it seems to me likely that will be done best if the dismissals take place at the week-end rather than near the beginning of the week'.*

He finished by saying *'let me know if you would like to expand on any of this in discussion.*

Yours sincerely, Geoffrey'.

5

The Call for Strike Action

On Monday 13th January, the building in Gray's Inn Road was buzzing following the announcement that *The Sunday Times Supplement* was to be printed at Wapping. By 10am, clerical shop stewards had been to the Advertising Accounts Department (AAD) where, normally, the job advertisements were fed into a computer. This work had been removed from the section and was being sent directly to Wapping, confirming the company's intentions for the following week's *Supplement*. The AAD Manager sending the work had previously been Deputy FOC of *The Times* clerical chapel. As in the Machine Room, the members concerned were angry but, with the mass meeting due that afternoon, and the ballot to follow, the order from union officials was that no action be taken.

On that same morning, the company gave employees at TNL and NGN six months' notice of termination of their contracts of employment. This applied to everyone except the journalists. It was clear that, after six months had elapsed, employees at Bouverie Street and Gray's Inn Road would be subject to *The London Post* agreement which outlawed union chapels, industrial action and the closed shop. If the workforce rejected the new contract, their work was sure to go to Wapping, where Murdoch would have six more months to prepare the ground.

The members reacted to these events with a mixture of anger and fear and these emotions were carried to the mass meeting. On the evening of Monday 13th January, the clerical members left work and boarded coaches which took them across London to the Academy Cinema in Brixton, where the meeting of SOGAT members from all four of Murdoch's titles was to be held. For many of them, it was the day they realized fully the seriousness of the situation they were facing.

The old Academy Cinema had been converted into a music venue, with the down-stairs seating stripped out to accommodate the Rock and Reggae fans. Many of the clerical people, surrounded by an elaborate but down at heel décor, squeezed into seats in the packed circle. They looked down on the stage where Brenda Dean, flanked by members of the National Executive Committee and other union officials, faced a sea of printers standing in the open stalls. In all, some 4,000 people crammed into the old building which, on a bitterly cold night, had no heating at all.

The National Executive meeting of the 10th December had endorsed the proposal that there should be a mass meeting of all members, followed immediately by a ballot asking the membership to give the Executive a mandate to take whatever industrial action they thought necessary, including calling a strike.

Brenda Dean believed she could use this threat to reach a negotiated settlement with Murdoch. Her opening address consisted of a history of the establishment of the Wapping plant and the negotiations surrounding it, including a veiled attack on the branches for not taking action in early September when dummy copies of a paper almost identical to *The Sun* were produced there. She explained the role played by the EETPU, describing it as 'despicable', and went on to say that there were three ways to proceed:

'The first way will be to accept everything the company wants. There will be a lot of people who will not even be given the chance to go to Wapping, maybe because they don't have blue eyes or some other such reason.

The second way is to be the house-trained pet that we have been for the last six months. To co-operate, get the extra papers out, smile when we are looked at. What will happen then? You will go to work one night and there will be no *Sun* in Bouverie Street and no *Times* in Gray's Inn Road, because they will have been transferred to Wapping. We either hit them now or we do not hit them at all!

The third way is to get off our knees, to stop being house-trained pets and to refuse to accept that we are going to be shackled. We have dignity as human beings and Murdoch is going to have to recognize that. We either get off our knees and fight, or continue until you haven't got a job.

I will conclude by saying this: those are the three ways. We have tried the first: we tried negotiating and we are still trying to negotiate. We tried the second way following the incident of 5th September 1985 (a dummy run) and we worked normally. We have not tried the third way, that is, to stand up and fight.

Your Executive Council has chosen which way they want to go and they want you with them and on this one it is the union, it is not a case of fighting for the union, you, as individuals, are the union. We have too much respect for you as members to lead you down a blind alley. I say to you vote "Yes" on the ballot paper.'

Contributions from the floor were dominated by the Machine Branch FOCs and their deputies, with speaker after speaker making the same belligerent 'let's take him on' speech. Of the 22 contributions, only two came from the clerical chapels. Cheryl Yanowitz, a secretary from *The News of the World*, proposed that the strike should involve the rest of Fleet Street and George Hall, News Group FOC, said, 'we know if there is a fight, the fight is for all of us. There are 900 clerical members employed by TNL and News Group. Murdoch has already recruited copytakers, telesales, accounts ... We will sacrifice everything, but Brenda, please don't sacrifice us'.

In her summing up Brenda Dean, in answer to George's plea said: 'I will try to take that in the spirit which I believe it was meant. We will do our very best in this dispute. We expect everyone to face up to their responsibilities. We are in this together, or we are not in it at all.'

Oblique reference was made to the possibility of the union being sequestrated when it was stated that the National Executive Council had taken into account that a dispute would, at some stage, bring the union into conflict with the law, but no indication was given as to what might happen when that time came.

For many, the information received at the meeting had confirmed their worst fears about the seriousness of the situation but, as they streamed out onto the street to be met by arc lights and television cameras, the old anxiety was tempered by a new mood of determination. The job now was to convince those who had not attended the meeting to vote 'Yes' on the ballot paper.

Mick: *There must have been 4,000 people at the Brixton meeting, all very excited and putting our trust in Brenda. It was dominated by the machine chapels and I was annoyed that we didn't get a look in. But I listened to them because, at the time, it was all I wanted to hear. I wouldn't accept what was happening to us and I wanted to strike. Everyone who got up was in favour of striking, there wasn't one speaker against.*

Denise: *What struck me about the Brixton meeting was how the machine men were so enamoured with Brenda. I remember her speech: 'We won't let you down ... We are not going to be house-trained poodles ...'*

Pam: *All the Machine Branch speakers were wading in and building up a real hype for the strike. They were just working themselves up. Backing each other up and saying the same things over and over again. What the clerical people said was much more to the point, much more lucid. But I thought: 'With this sort of fervour, we can't fail to win'.*

41

Carmel: *I was disgusted with the meeting. Nearly all of the TNL clerical chapel were sitting in the balcony and had no chance of getting to the microphone. I wanted to speak against going on strike. I wanted to propose that we should stop all casual or temporary working and impose an overtime ban at the four titles. I voted against going on strike.*

Ballot forms were issued on 14th January and called for industrial action unless there was a guarantee from the company of continuity of employment, with no compulsory redundancies if any of the papers moved to Wapping. On the same day, the EETPU showed its contempt for the other unions and their members when it announced that it had no objections to negotiating with Murdoch over Wapping, disregarding the instruction from Norman Willis that no separate agreements should be made with the company.

The threatened supplement was duly printed at Wapping on Sunday 19th January. Once again, production continued at Bouverie Street and Gray's Inn Road despite the fact that agreements had been broken by the company once the supplement had appeared. The main body of the paper, printed at Gray's Inn Road, contained a 12-page 'Innovation Special – The Future of Fleet Street' which began:

'This weekend saw a landmark in British newspaper publishing when the first copies of a new fourth section of *The Sunday Times* rolled off the printing presses of News International's spectacular new £100 million plant at Wapping, near London's Tower Bridge. The commissioning of Wapping has allowed *The Sunday Times* to break free of traditional production constraints to publish Britain's biggest ever newspaper. Wapping is the face of Fleet Street to come. It combines the latest in high-tech production, with the best in modern labour practices. The result will be bigger and better newspapers for readers and advertisers and secure, well-paid jobs for those who produce them. This 12-page 'Innovation Special' looks at the technology involved and at the implications, beginning with an in-depth interview with Rupert Murdoch, chairman of News International.'

Murdoch said that his original plan was for a second printing plant at Wapping which would produce extra copies of *The Sun* and *The News of the World*. He admitted that the company 'came close' to agreement with *The News of the World* machine room chapel but 'subsequently, we decided that the only way to bring the plant into production was to treat it as a Greenfield site and staff it with people outside the existing Fleet Street workforce, to start a London evening paper'.

Later, the interviewer referred to the central issue of disagreement with the unions: Murdoch's insistence that his workforce be denied the right to withdraw their labour in the event of a legitimate dispute. 'I am convinced', he said, 'there can be no security for our business and for our newspapers, and all that that means both to their employees and their readers, without a certainty of production.'

Asked if the company could distribute their newspapers without SOGAT, Murdoch replied: 'Oh yes, that's the least of our problems. We hope it doesn't come to this, but we have contingency plans to distribute all our newspapers to every retailer in the country direct, by 6am every morning of the year.'

Have you got the capacity to print all four titles: *The Sun, News of the World, The Times* and *Sunday Times* at Wapping? 'We don't want to do that because, of course, we don't have sufficient presses to do that satisfactorily. We want to start *The Post* there and we want to put work there as we grow out of our existing two plants. But if we are struck in the manner in which the unions are now threatening, then we will have no choice but to try and keep producing as best we can.'

What happens in the unlikely situation that the unions don't strike? What if they are, as has been suggested, prepared to let you go your own way at Wapping, while they sit tight in Gray's Inn Road and Bouverie Street? 'Well, my fingers are crossed. Of course, we would then have to negotiate house agreements that are coming up and try to get improved efficiencies in the existing two plants. We are looking for security of production, greater capacity, modern competitive costs and flexible working practices'.

This edition of *The Sunday Times* was the last to be printed on the Gray's Inn Road presses.

On Tuesday 21st January, the result of the ballot of SOGAT members was announced, with 3,534 votes in favour of industrial action and 752 against There had been a 90% turnout and of those who had voted, over 80% were in favour, with the clerical chapels voting 520 to 190 for the strike. The NGA, who had also held a ballot for industrial action, announced on the same day a vote in favour by 843 to 117. Armed with these results, Brenda Dean announced that she was to have one last attempt at a negotiated settlement with the company.

With strike action imminent, Clerical Branch officials met to discuss plans for financial support for the strikers, including a levy of all members, which would be vital to ensure a minimum level of strike pay. Because of a continuing belief that Murdoch would not be able to produce and distribute the papers from Wapping, there was no discussion about clerical workers at the other newspapers handling the News International titles at their place of work.

On Thursday 23rd, *The Sun* journalists, bribed with a £2,000 per head payout from the company, disobeyed an instruction by their union and voted by 100 to 8 to transfer to Wapping. In addition, the electricians employed at NGN and TNL, who had not been involved with the deception at Wapping, were instructed by their union executive to cross picket lines at Bouverie Street and Gray's Inn Road. It was also the final day of negotiations between News International and the unions.

Murdoch made it clear from the outset that he was not there to talk about the new plant. 'The horse has bolted at Wapping' he said. He also referred to the recent agreements between Brenda Dean and Maxwell, including her acceptance of 2000 redundancies. She responded by saying he could have the same deal, but he didn't reply. Murdoch also made it clear that he intended to introduce the same terms and conditions at Gray's Inn Road and Bouverie Street that he had proposed for *The London Post*.

Then, in an effort to ensure a deal, concessions were given which went a lot further than those given to Maxwell. Brenda Dean outlined an offer, worked out with the other unions, which conceded management's right to manage, agreed to binding arbitration on any dispute, gave flexibility between unions, prohibited wildcat strikes and promised ballots before strikes. Murdoch responded by insisting 'If this had come three months ago, the answer might have been yes'. The offer from the unions came just 10 days after the meeting at Brixton at which Brenda Dean had passionately implored her members to 'get off your knees and fight'.

At the final session of the talks, Murdoch stated: 'I reject any recognition for your members at Tower Hamlets,' put his hands on the table and pushed his chair back. At that moment, the talks ended and the gains made by the unions over many years were about to be eradicated.

It was reported at lunch-time that negotiations had broken down and, amid a clamour of reporters and exploding flashlights, Murdoch put the blame squarely at the door of the unions, while stressing his benevolence towards his workforce. He also made great play over the unions' capitulation at Mirror Group, stating that they 'seem to roll over and play dead for Mr Maxwell', even though Brenda Dean had offered him the same deal just a few hours earlier.

6

On Strike

As news of the breakdown of talks reached Gray's Inn Road, clerical chapel representatives were made aware that a number of employees had expressed their willingness to cross picket lines and carry on working. Although the majority of the chapel appeared to be firm, there was some anxiety that the 'scabs' might influence those who still had doubts. It was vital, therefore, that the chapel meeting, arranged for lunch-time on the 24th, proclaimed a clear and optimistic message.

The meeting was very positive, with some shop stewards challenging those who were considering crossing the lines to state their reasons. No one responded. Despite the uncertainty surrounding the future, the meeting ended with a strong mood of unity.

During the afternoon, employees at Gray's Inn Road got their first glimpse of the role the law was to play in the dispute. At 3 o'clock, van loads of police arrived outside the building, cleared all the parked vehicles and erected metal barriers around its perimeter. The company, in complicity with the police, was preparing for the strike.

All chapel officials from NGN and TNL were called to a meeting at SOGAT Central Branch offices in Britannia Street, near Kings Cross Station, at 5.30pm. The 70 or so representatives listened attentively as Brenda Dean took them through the events of the previous day. She mentioned Murdoch's statement about the unions rolling over and playing dead for Maxwell, slipping in the fact that she had offered Murdoch the very same deal. Surprisingly, when it came to questions, no one mentioned the fact that she had been willing to give one third redundancies among all the other abhorrent aspects of the Maxwell deal. At that time, many of those present were unaware that considerably more had been offered to Murdoch at the final meeting.

Very little was planned at this stage in the way of picketing. It was still the general feeling that once the presses stopped rolling at Bouverie Street and Gray's Inn Road, the company would want to restart negotiations. At 6.40pm, Brenda Dean formally announced that the strike had begun and the clerical reps returned to Gray's Inn Road and Bouverie Street to inform their members.

John: *We were approached by the Industrial Relations Manager, who kept demanding, 'Are you on strike? Will you leave the building?' He had been an FOC at the* Financial Times, *sitting on the branch committee for many years, and served as a Labour Councillor. Now, here he was, one of Murdoch's men. We told him to shove off.*

Although the strike was only 20 minutes old, people were escorted off the premises and given a letter which read:

'Dear Sir/Madam,
The industrial action in which you have participated today has disrupted production of the company's titles.

By participating in that industrial action you have been and are in repudiatory breach of your contract of employment. The company accepts your breach as terminating your employment with immediate effect. It is also accepting breaches of contract by other employees participating in the industrial action as terminating their employment.

Your employment having ended, your P45 and any money due will follow shortly.'

John: *Having informed our members that the strike was on, I went down to the Machine Room. It was deserted, with not a sound to be heard. Word of the strike had obviously spread very quickly and there was no sign of any activity. I went to leave the building through the back entrance, which leads from the Machine Room out into Gough Street, but discovered a bloke welding the lock on the big double gates. I remember thinking that the company was going to some lengths to make sure we were not going to get back in. That turned out to be something of an underestimation.*

Joyce: *When Helen was about 18 months, I got in touch with Caxton House, the Head Office of the London Clerical Branch. I started doing Saturday shifts and the odd day in the week at the* Sunday Times. *I did a few Saturdays and then someone went sick and they said, 'Can't you get somebody to have your kids. It's only a four-day week and it would be some more money for you'. I did that and they were brilliant to me. People had holidays and someone might have been sick or something. I'll never forget that, those girls kept me in work.*

I was a Temp and I could have gone out and got other temp work, but I stuck with the dispute because they were my people. They had kept my family fed for eight months. They were all magic, apart from one or two exceptions, and there was absolutely no question of not being supportive to the chapel. Then there was a meeting and the Temps were told they could stay with it if they wanted to and a whole group of us stayed.

When we came out of the building I had a row with a paper seller from Militant *who was on the door-step. They deserve it. It's just a game to them. They're all young and earnest. I was young and earnest once. But we were going to be out of work.*

What Murdoch did stank, it was appalling and I knew I must support the strike. It never occurred to me not to be involved. It was great to be taken into a chapel like that.

We eventually got strike pay and people looked after us. As the dispute went on I got to know people. Being a copy-taker meant being shut away in a little room, I hardly knew anybody outside my department. I made some good mates during the strike.

Frank: *I can honestly say that I loved my job. To some people it's just 9 to 5, pick up your pay packet on a Friday and enjoy your evenings and weekends. But I had the freedom of the building from down in the Press Room, right up to the managerial floor and I knew virtually everybody in the company. It was very interesting and I loved it. In return for that, I didn't begrudge the time. I may have spent the best part of the day out of the office, meeting people and dealing with their problems. Or out with a Rep, or visiting some factory or other and, at the end of the day I'd think to myself, 'well, if somebody walked in now and asked me what I've done today, I've got very little to show for it'. There were all the orders to prepare after the day's happenings so, quite voluntary, I would stay in the evening and prepare them ready to be typed up and sent off the next morning. Because I loved the job, I gave it no end of my own time.*

During the week prior to the, as you might say, 'outbreak of war', I believed that if the strike were to happen it could mean the end of my job. I went into it fully aware that we were laying our jobs on the line. A lot of people may have thought, as in the past, that it was just another dispute, that there'd be a settlement and we'd all walk back later on. But I never did believe that.

On the last Friday we were there TM, my immediate boss as Office Services Manager, came over to me and simply said, 'I take it you'll be toeing the line'. Not, 'what are you going to do?' or 'will you be coming in'. I suppose, over a period of time, he had worked out my sympathies. He caught me round at the sink washing up some cups, a sort of off-guard moment, and I simply said 'Yes'. He went into business straightaway and asked me some questions about the stores. I couldn't refuse really, so I said 'Ok'.

It was rather strange because on that Friday I was actually going out for the evening. For a long, long time I'd drifted away from going to the theatre, I had really become so immersed in my job that it had taken over. I went for ages, years really, with virtually no social life, but it just happened that I had booked seats for that Friday night. Normally, I would have stayed on fairly late but, at 5.30,

47

I chucked a few things in a plastic bag and just walked out. I'd been at The Times *27 years.*

Deirdre: *On the Friday night the strike started I was booking ads for the following week and telling clients they were wasting their time because there wasn't going to be a paper next week. I really didn't think there would be, certainly not a paper worth talking about. But the information the national union gave us was really bad and had we known the true story, the capacity the plant had, I think we would have used different tactics. I don't think there would have been a majority for a strike and we would have been more of a nuisance staying at work.*

Michele: *The tension was unbearable. I cleared my desk on the Friday evening and there were a few journalists left. They didn't have anything to say to me, they seemed quite willing to see me go out the door without saying a word. I said goodbye to Derek Collier, who I had a lot of respect for, and he said, 'oh, don't worry, it's all a storm in a teacup. You'll be back on Monday. Nothing's happening'.*

After the strike call on Friday 24th January, contingency plans were put into action and on the following morning a number of clerical activists picketed *The Sunday Times* building in Gray's Inn Road. *The Sun* and *The Times* had not been printed on the previous evening and despite the decision by *The Sun* journalists to go to Wapping on the previous day, the mood was fairly positive. Not many clerical people worked on Saturdays, but the company had worked hard to ensure that their managerial staff broke ranks with the strike and managers from the Correspondence and Tele Ads departments, along with a number of their staff, chose to 'scab', either arriving very early in the morning, or using rear entrances to the building to avoid the pickets.

Around noon, several clerical chapel committee members arrived, charged with the task of clearing the chapel administration's belongings from the 'offices' situated on the roof of the *Sunday Times* building. They were let in and escorted to the sixth floor by the security staff, all union members, who explained that they were unable, legally, to leave the building and join the strike. Many of the chapel files had been transferred to the Branch offices during the previous week, but there was still furniture, filing cabinets, typewriters and computer equipment to be carried along the catwalks that crossed the roof.

John: *I was feeling in a pretty sombre mood, seeing the chapel offices being emptied and thinking it could be my last time in the building, when Andrew*

Neil, Editor of The Sunday Times, *burst through the swing doors near the lift. 'You're not leaving us are you?' he said with a huge smirk on his face. I said something rude and he turned and fled. In hindsight, I wish I'd throttled him. He was responsible for so much misery.*

On Saturday afternoon, the TNL and NGN chapel committees congregated at the clerical branch headquarters at Caxton House in South London to meet for the first time since the strike began. They devised a framework for staffing an Operations Room, a 'nerve-centre' for the strike and, bearing in mind that it was January, made arrangements for the pickets to be supplied with hot tea and rolls. A steady flow of people would be needed to staff the picket lines, but rotas could not be drawn up until all the members were gathered together for the first joint chapel meeting on the following Monday. So a telephone tree was set up to ensure that as many people as possible turned out on the picket lines first thing Monday morning.

At this stage, the clerical pickets were only being organized for the Gray's Inn Road and Bouverie Street buildings as it was felt that the company would not have made arrangements for those who were willing to ignore the strike call to arrive at the Wapping plant on the first day.

Carmel: *I went to Caxton House for the committee meeting and then stayed to help set up the Operations Room. In the evening a group of us started phoning in false copy to the telephone reporters departments at Wapping and at Gray's Inn Road. We read out articles from old newspapers and just kept bombarding them. The following morning we got hold of a copy of* The Sunday Times *and there were quite a few large blank spaces in it.*

There had been no call by the national unions, or the London branches, for picketing to take place at Wapping on the Saturday evening and only a few hundred people turned up at the plant. Indeed, on that evening, many of the clerical activists from TNL were at a farewell party for one of their committee members who was about to emigrate to New Zealand.

In their desperation to gain recognition at Wapping, the national unions had offered Murdoch everything they thought he wanted. Having rejected that offer, their hope now was that he would not be able to produce or distribute the papers. As the strike commenced, SOGAT issued an instruction to its members in the wholesale distribution depots across the country not to handle the News International titles.

Those present at Wapping that evening, however, saw a large police presence at the front of the plant and a steady stream of articulated lorries and white vans leaving the building. These vehicles were owned by TNT and the majority of their drivers were members of the Transport and General Workers' Union (TGWU). A few days later, the TGWU issued an instruction to its members driving TNT lorries not to cross the print-workers picket lines. On the same day, News International gained an injunction from the High Court ordering the TGWU to lift its instructions to the drivers. Fearing a heavy fine or sequestration, the union duly capitulated.

At shortly after seven o'clock on the morning of Monday 27th, pickets began arriving at Gray's Inn Road and the mood, despite the momentous events of the weekend, was optimistic: The company had succeeded in producing all four titles at Wapping on the previous two nights and distributed the papers by road to the newsagents. On the previous day the journalists at *The Times* agreed to work at the new plant. They were to be followed by *Sunday Times* journalists who, on the afternoon of the 27th, voted by 68 to 60 to move to Wapping. As they travelled by bus and tube to Grays Inn Road, the pickets read the front-page headline of *The Sun* over the shoulders of the early commuters. It was the first edition to come out of Wapping and it read: 'A NEW SUN IS RISING TODAY – We beat strike thugs'.

By 8.30, there were some 100 clerical pickets outside *The Sunday Times*. (*The Times* building, which was joined to *The Sunday Times* by a foot-bridge at third floor level, was locked, and only a token presence was kept on the door.) People were placed at various entrances around the building in case the scabs attempted to sneak in unseen, but rumours that the company had laid on coaches to 'bus' workers in via the underground car park, proved to be unfounded. By 10 o'clock, about 100 clerical members – 20% of the chapel – had crossed the picket lines. As on the Saturday, many were department managers, but nearly all of the telephone advertising department went into work. A handful of wobblers were persuaded to stick with the strike, but many more were unwilling to listen to the pleas of their former workmates.

John: *We had a handful of committee members and a few other chapel members at Gray's Inn Road on the Saturday, the first full day of the strike, but* we got the word around and set up a picket line on Monday. The whole thing seemed so well planned by the management that we wondered if they had arranged to use different entrances, so we had pickets down in the van ways and elsewhere. People I remember being very placid at work had so much anger when they saw their former colleagues crossing the line and pickets were allowed to get away with things on the first days that the police didn't allow later. There was a column of strikers on either side of the entrance and the scabs had to run the gauntlet as they came in.

There was some real anger. Some of the scabs were very cocky about what they were doing and a couple of people on our side snapped. Someone going in made a flippant remark and the lad next to me said, 'well, if you're going in, get in', and booted him up the back-side and through the swing doors. A policewoman came over and ticked him off. If that incident had happened a few weeks later he would have been arrested and charged with assault.

From the picket at Gray's Inn Road, we went on to the Conway Hall, in Holborn, for our first joint chapel meeting with The Sun people. We had met their committee on the previous Saturday and gone through the plans for the strike. By Monday, half a dozen of them had gone in! In all about 40% of News Group's 300 clerical members had crossed the picket line.

The main object of the meeting was to get people involved in the dispute straightaway. There were many things to be done: the chapels would have to be run from the Branch offices at Caxton House and we had to get picket rotas set up. We had 60 to 70 volunteers for picket duty that afternoon and we went straight back to Gray's Inn Road where news filtered through later on in the day that News International had obtained a court order against SOGAT to lift the instruction to its members in the wholesale distribution depots not to handle the company's titles. It was noted on the picket line how quickly the courts could operate when a person such as Murdoch needed them to make a decision on his behalf.

Tim: *I went on the picket line at Gray's Inn Road on the Saturday. Most of us were there again at eight on Monday morning and I stayed until eight o'clock that night. I slept at Caxton House and did the same on Tuesday and Wednesday and went home on Thursday. I was back again on Friday. Very few of the people going to work would talk to us, but the exception was a secretary. She was visibly upset and said there was a bad atmosphere inside the building. During the first days things were definitely better outside than in.*

Graham: *In September '85, there had been a chapel meeting at the Friends Meeting House at Euston and everybody from the Library had gone except those who, eventually, were to go into work when the strike began. I wonder now if they had been told in advance what was going on. Over the weekend following the strike announcement, individual members of the Library staff were telephoned at home and asked to break the strike by going into work on Monday morning. One or two did approach the building with the intention of going in, but were stopped at the door by their colleagues who persuaded them not to.*

Tim: *In my department, only four of us out of eight came out and at the first TNL/NGN chapel meeting on the Monday morning, we heard that 40% had crossed the picket lines at News Group.*

John: *One person I knew must have had every intention of going in because he turned up on that first morning with his squash gear, all ready for a game at lunch-time. I said, 'you're not going in are you Bob?' and he said, 'yes, what's the point?' 'Go and walk past Marie (a woman who worked in his department) and tell her you're going in', I said. But he couldn't do it.*

Frank: *The main topic of conversation outside the building in Gray's Inn Road during the first few days concerned who had gone into work and I was sickened that so many people I had worked with during my 27 years had gone in. People on my management level had almost all continued to work, there were only a half dozen who came out.*

I found it difficult on the picket line. In fact, I didn't engage in any verbal abuse, because I couldn't bring myself to do it. But as much as I felt absolute contempt for those people who went in – and when I was at Gray's Inn Road and saw them going in I did feel almost hatred for them – you can't just alter your nature and I couldn't indulge in running across the road and confronting them and so on. But it didn't embarrass me when people did those things, in fact, I rather applauded their courage in doing what I could not bring myself to do.

Some of the chaps from the Addressograph Department spoke to their ex-boss and said to him: 'why are you doing this?' His reply was, 'I'm not going to chuck away 30 years just like that'. I imagine that was the attitude of a lot of the longer-serving people, my contemporaries. 'I've got a reasonable position and the perks that go with it. I'm not going to give it all up now'.

7

The Journalists

The National Union of Journalists decided at national level that it would have nothing to do with Wapping until News International reached agreement with the print unions. This was fine in theory, but not enough work was put in to convince members working on Murdoch's papers. Instead, the company was allowed to spread rumours, talking loosely about a possible £8,000 pay-off, plus a 25% increase in salaries, if they moved to the new plant. As the seriousness of the situation became clearer during the month leading up to the dispute, all the unions represented at *The Times* and the *Sunday Times* met on a regular basis. It soon became very apparent that the journalists were having a great deal of difficulty holding their membership together and the FOC of *The Sunday Times* resigned a week before the dispute started.

Denise: *I remember Greg Neal,* The Times *NUJ FOC, asking me what had happened at our meeting and I said, 'I'm not going to tell you, 'cause we all know what you're going to do', and he just laughed.*

Traditionally, the journalists saw the printers' practices as an obstacle in getting their stories out and there was a great deal of jealousy because the printers were earning as much, if not more, than they were earning themselves. Their attitude of superiority, expressed in phrases like 'we are *The Times*', was something that many clerical workers experienced in their day to day contact with journalists, although it should be stressed that not everyone showed this arrogance.

Graham: *On 24ᵗʰ January, as on any other Friday, there was a steady flow of journalists into the library. But there was something different about them as they aimlessly turned the pages of newspaper files or asked for clippings and information. They had vacant, bewildered expressions and appeared to have something else on their minds. Then someone blurted it out. Murdoch had given them an ultimatum: either accept £2,000 and free membership of BUPA to go to Wapping, or be sacked.*
 Their first reaction was one of disbelief, after all, they were journalists. How

could he treat them as he treated everyone else? Then came the fear: 'I've got a wife and kids to support'. 'How would I pay my mortgage?' Only one of them, Brian Dear, showed any sign of resistance and he was dismayed by his colleagues' attitudes. 'I can't believe it', he said, 'but I think they're going to go'.

With a few honourable exceptions, they did go. Their capitulation was a major victory for Murdoch and had a devastating effect on the course of the dispute. *The Times* and *The Sunday Times* continued to be published and any resistance to Murdoch's interference in the content of the papers was effectively removed.

They tried, later, to cover their tracks with lame justifications: Peter Wilby of *The Sunday Times* and former NUJ FOC held out for a week and wrote an article for *New Socialist* in which he tried to explain why he finally gave in. 'I'm not sure it will convince me', he wrote, 'let alone anyone else'.

> 'Like the vast majority of *The Sunday Times* journalists, I dislike the print unions. On a paper like ours, next Sunday's article may be a culmination of weeks (even months) of research. It is only human to resent a threat to its appearance created by one of the National Graphical Association's interminable demands for extra machine room manning. I have a certain grudging admiration for the unions' success in preserving their members' jobs, at high wages for so long. But they have often behaved more like capitalist labour contractors than trade unions.
>
> But recognition of the unions' shortcomings was one thing, support for Murdoch's solutions quite another. Since October, he has seemed hell-bent not on forcing realistic negotiations on manning levels and new technology, but on sacking some 5,000 people and starting afresh. These were not the abstractions of manning levels: they included secretaries, librarians, messengers and copy-takers – my friends and colleagues. We journalists, I suppose, expected gentler treatment.
>
> *The Sunday Times* NUJ chapel met on Monday 27th January to consider the ultimatum. As is now well known, it voted 68-60 to accept the move to Wapping ... for most of us it was the first (probably the only) time in our lives that we faced a moral and political choice from which there was no escape ...
>
> In a property owning democracy, the price of the average citizen's soul is a little less than the cost of his or her mortgage.'

At least Peter Wilby was honest enough to admit that they had failed to rise to the challenge. Clifford Longley, Religious Affairs correspondent of *The Times*, wrote that

> 'news must get through ... it drives us now, and it is nothing to do with the character of a particular employer. Journalists believe in journalism and

are near-addicted to the daily charge of adrenalin it brings and we, of all journalists, are conditioned to even-handedness, to seeing every side of every argument, and to the professional detachment which gives us the automatic habit of non-involvement in other people's crises.'

But this was not someone else's crisis. The journalists, like it or not, were participants, not observers, and their stated belief in their profession, above all else, was an excuse to side-step the issue and divert criticism. If his house was broken into, would Clifford Longley plead, 'I'm a journalist' and stand by taking notes?

Among the pickets at Wapping, the journalists were considered at best, spineless and at worst, hostile to the cause and the animosity directed towards them was forthright. Many were recognized as they made their way into the plant and their names were chanted along with the cries of 'scab'. This was considered a legitimate response by the strikers and it was done without shame, to make their experience of crossing the picket lines and going into work a thoroughly unpleasant one. It must be admitted, however, that some people sank to using personal and racist insults, which gave journalists such as Bernard Levin the opportunity to score points by alleging the worst kind of anti-Semitic abuse. This did our cause nothing but harm.

During the course of the dispute a number of journalists left Wapping, citing either their conscience or the pressures of working at the plant. In June, NUJ members from *The Sun* decided to hold a ballot on whether they should continue to work at the new plant. This gave the strikers some valuable propaganda regarding the demoralization of the staff inside Wapping and when NUJ members from other newspapers picketed the main gate, six of *The Sun* journalists did not cross the picket line. The strikers, however, remained cynical about the outcome of the ballot, having watched their own picket lines crossed with impunity for five months and, sure enough, when Murdoch offered them a 10% pay rise, only six voted to stop working.

In the same month the NUJ held a ballot of its members at *The Times* calling for strike action in support of their colleagues who had been sacked for refusing to work at Wapping. The NUJ were insisting that the eight should be suspended without pay whilst their cases were dealt with through the normal disputes procedure which included the involvement of the conciliation service ACAS.

In a very low turn-out, *The Times* chapel voted by a majority of 2 to 1 not to take any action in support of their former colleagues.

The truth?
He couldn't give
a XXXX

8

Picketing

Tim: *Picketing was something you really wanted to get involved in. We hadn't done anything wrong, I didn't want any more money, or to change my job and I was quite prepared to carry on in whatever building it was. For someone to come along and say I was worthless, just a piece of junk, was too much for me.*

The picketing was soon organized on a rota basis, with the different unions and branches allocated specific duty times. From 3pm to 7pm, six clerical pickets were to stand behind the barriers across the road from *The Sunday Times* building, supporting the Machine Branch people on the door. At least, it was thought they were machine branch people. (With most of the clerical staff working 'office hours' and those working on the presses doing 'night shifts' the two groups of workers had had little contact with each other before they were sacked).

These were ghostly men, disappearing two or three at a time for 'a quick cuppa', or tramping off *en masse* to the inevitable meeting. Sometimes they would turn up again later (much later) on the next corner, or just stroll by with a patronizing nod. So the clericals stood there – for four hours at a time – in front of the glass doors plastered with strike stickers and posters, surrounded by policemen and black dustbin bags overflowing with half-eaten sandwiches and plastic tea cups; stamping their freezing feet on dog-ends and discarded copies of *The Evening Standard* dropped off by the delivery van drivers and eagerly awaited by the pickets who would read *anything* to relieve the tedium.

Graham: *On one occasion I was knocked flying by an unusually aggressive motor cycle messenger who was going into the building (most of these just said lamely that they would be sacked if they didn't cross the picket line, which was probably true) and was threatened by the senior police officer on duty: 'stand in front of the doors again and you're nicked' he said.*

After the sequestration judgment, they would not even permit us to use 'offensive' terms like 'scab'. It made no difference that we were deeply offended every time someone crossed our picket line, undermining our efforts to win back our jobs. And every instruction from the police was accompanied by the threat of arrest.

It would have been easy, apart from the cold and discomfort, to just stand there as far away from the door and the policemen as one could without losing all credibility. It was hard to continually confront those going in and out – the journalists and managers, the messengers and taxi drivers and your ex-colleagues – to challenge them and make them consider their actions without resorting to the same tired name-calling. You tried because you believed you were right and because you didn't want to let anyone down. I began by asking them not to cross. If they insisted, and I only recall one person turning back in twelve months, I asked them why. Almost everyone just brushed past, but it was some small compensation to watch them pushing all the wrong swing doors in a frantic effort to avoid the issue and get inside.

A smartly dressed woman with a briefcase actually stopped one afternoon and we had a short discussion about the rights and wrongs of her going in. The next time I saw her, she was leaving the building with a boy of nine or ten and someone shouted 'scab'. She clutched the child to her breast in an exaggerated show of protection and looked straight at me. Her hurt expression quickly turned to disdain and then to sheer loathing. It's uncomfortable when you realise that someone despises you and I had to remind myself that I wasn't something that had just crawled out of the gutter. Then I was angry that she should shift the guilt and I shouted after her that it was my children who were really suffering – through her actions – and not her child suffering through mine. The look on her face still haunts me – and it still makes me angry.

To harangue one's former workmates did not require the same self-motivation – it was personal, and we did things we could not have imagined ourselves doing before the strike. On one occasion my fellow pickets and I – librarians male and female – followed two former colleagues along Gray's Inn Road, shouting after them. Eventually, after about half a mile, one of the younger among us caught up with the pair. He was much smaller than either, but was so angry that he barged into them and when I arrived on the scene a few moments later, they were ashen-faced and hurriedly climbing into a cab to make their escape. Even as we were following them I remember being surprised at what we were doing. But the circumstances were not normal. They had disregarded the democratic decision to strike for their own gain, our jobs had been hijacked and our situation was desperate. Not one of them could look you in the eye, but as time passed and they crossed the picket lines day after day, the realization dawned that they were not going to change their minds.

When it got too cold, or too boring, or too depressing, we took it in turns to go to the caff where we discussed the strike endlessly over cups of tea, swapping tit-bits of hearsay and scouring the papers for snippets of information, desperate for any crumb of comfort. But throughout the whole year of the strike, I don't recall anything, anything at all, that gave us cause for real optimism.

Denise: *It was freezing when I went on my first picket duty and it took me ages to get up the Gray's Inn Road in my moon boots and layers of clothes. I didn't see anyone I knew coming out of the building and very few people at all, but I was standing on the door when a chap walked past me and one of the policemen said, 'go on, why don't you have a go at him?' They were laughing and joking with us, but their attitude changed later on.*

It must have been terrible knowing you had to go to work and face the pickets. 'Who's going to be there today, will it be someone I know? Is it going to be a mass picket? Should I go in early to avoid the crowd, or later when there may be fewer of them?' They had to walk from the station not knowing who they might meet on the way. Then, having got into work, not daring to go out at lunch-time and worrying all day about getting out again in the evening. They had to grit their teeth and walk past people they had worked with for maybe twenty years and I don't see how anyone could be unaffected by that. The Chief Librarian actually hid in the tobacconist's on the corner. To revert to crouching in shops and hiding! Apparently, someone was making threatening phone calls to strikers' homes saying, 'If you don't stop picketing I'll get you.'

Although I don't know of anyone who actually changed their mind and stopped going in, some certainly didn't appear for work for a number of weeks. There was a great deal of 'sickness'. Others took the money, applied for redundancy and got it. Perhaps if we hadn't picketed the way we did, they would have carried on.

Joyce: *On one occasion I had the kids down there at tea-time. The aggravation of picketing with children nobody can fathom. I had to carry Helen and it was cold. She was two and Sean was four.*

I get told I've indoctrinated my children, but this is what happened to us. Sean loved the picket line. I remember lifting him up at one of the big meetings at Westminster Central Hall when Brenda came in. I was upstairs in the balcony and I shouted out, 'he's been on the picket line more than you'.

Graham: *The canteen staff at Gray's Inn Road were not employees of* The Times, *but worked for an outside catering firm. The pickets had mixed feelings about people who were helping the company to function, but probably faced the sack if they refused to cross the picket line. Sometimes they took pity on the pickets and sent out some cheese rolls or cups of tea.*

There was one striker, I think he belonged to the RIRMA branch, who often turned up on his bike while we were picketing the building. I'd first seen him at Wapping where, from a safe distance, he would harangue the police. He was just as vocal at Gray's Inn Road, always challenging people and getting more and more animated as the weeks passed. But when a motor cycle messenger retaliated physically one day, he became very nervous and agitated, squaring up and backing off all at the same time.

One afternoon a kindly chef appeared at the door carrying a huge silver platter piled high with little sandwiches which must have been leftovers from some management function. This was too much for the RIRMA man, who struck the tray with such force that dozens of sandwiches flew into the air and landed all over the chef who had fallen on his back in the doorway. Before the attendant policemen could move, the RIRMA man shot up the road, darted deftly through the traffic and disappeared. We all denied ever having seen him before and a couple of hours later, after the police had changed shifts, he came back for his bike. 'Did you see what I did to the sandwiches?' he asked everyone, well out of earshot of the police.

A number of people continued to work at Priory House, just off the Clerkenwell Road, where The Times Literary *and* Educational Supplements *were based. It was, perhaps, the worst of all the picket duties. The building stood at the top of St John Street, a narrow lane running from a medieval arch down to Smithfield Market. A nagging wind whistled constantly through the archway and the hapless pickets huddled in the corners and recesses of the old stonework. But there was no escape, it bit away at your legs no matter where you stood.*

Nothing ever happened at Priory House, it was four hours of misery. Few people went in and out of the building – which The Times *shared with other companies – and the pickets didn't know who were scabs and who weren't. When challenged, everybody denied that they worked for the paper.*

After a while you just gave up and stayed out of stubbornness and a naïve belief in the imminent arrival of the tea van. One freezing afternoon, a couple of us wandered into the headquarters of the Order of St John across the street, hoping that their exhibition about the history of the Order would provide a few minutes respite from the cold and boredom. But, just our luck, the exhibition was closed, so we contented ourselves in the foyer, casually reading the notice board, looking intently at the pictures around the walls and loitering by the radiator. It didn't last long though: a uniformed doorman delivered us smartly back outside.

From time to time, there were larger demonstrations at Gray's Inn Road, with two or three hundred people standing behind the barriers opposite The Sunday Times. *When a 'scab' was recognized approaching the building, his or her name would be shouted out and taken up by others in the crowd. The names of well know 'scabs', ex-union officials who had been 'bought off', managers who had instigated previous disputes, or were particularly disliked, would be chanted by everyone and sometimes aroused such anger and indignation that the barriers were swept aside as a great body of demonstrators, oblivious to the heavy traffic, surged across the street shouting 'scab, scab, scab'. There were racist and sexist remarks and people were spat on.*

These abuses gave the 'scabs' the excuse they needed to justify their actions and made them think of themselves as a small band of brave, persecuted souls. In truth, they were people without principle or integrity, many of them flouting a democratically taken decision to strike. Passive resistance never received serious consideration by the clerical chapels, let alone the machine branches. I wish it had. It would have taken a charismatic leader to have persuaded the strikers to adopt such a course, but I have to say that sadly, in the end, I don't believe it would have made any difference.

John: *We tried to turn the tables on them saying, 'Christ, you really look terrible. Is it me, or you, who's supposed to be suffering in this dispute?' One or two of them couldn't handle it and would start swearing and – on one occasion – the Chief Security Officer stormed out of the building shouting, 'get off my steps', as if he owned the place. We reported him to the police as a trouble maker!*

9

Fortress Wapping

Demonstrations were held at Wapping every Wednesday and Saturday night. The young left-wing paper sellers were usually the first arrivals at Tower Hill followed, in dribs and drabs, by the strikers, their families and supporters. The demonstrators were not difficult to spot: they were wrapped up against the cold and many wore the little enamel lapel badges struck to commemorate the strike, or the larger tin ones proclaiming: 'Don't Buy The Sun'. People chatted in small groups in the draughty entrance of Tower Hill tube station and on the pavement outside. Gradually, as their numbers swelled into the hundreds, the crowd spilled down the steps into the roadway and formed up loosely behind their union and political group banners, impatient to be under way. It took at least half an hour to cover the first few hundred yards to East Smithfield, where people in dinner jackets and evening gowns hurried off to the Tower Hotel, accompanied by the relentless call and response chanting of the marchers: 'Maggie – Out. Maggie – Out. Maggie, Maggie, Maggie – Out, Out, Out'.

Graham: *During the early weeks of the strike, turning up at Wapping on Saturday nights was optional. Only later, after a vote by the chapel, did it become compulsory. So I didn't go down initially because I was sceptical about the wisdom of mass picketing. I, like everyone else, had watched the television coverage of the miners' strike and though I sympathized wholeheartedly with their cause, I was disturbed by the violence. I can't remember why I changed my mind: the lack of any constructive alternative; simple curiosity; a feeling that I had a duty to be there, but, after a couple of weeks, I went.*

I got there at about nine in the evening and two things stick in my memory. One was the cold: it was bitter and I had so many clothes on I could hardly walk. The second was the policemen: I had never seen so many in my life! I met two work-mates and we had just gone into a pub for a tot of warming whisky, when two young women burst in though the door. One was supporting the other, who was clutching her face. She had been hit by one of the policemen, her teeth were broken and her mouth was cut and bleeding. Her companion helped her

◀ *Spiked railings, razor wire and security cameras around the perimeter of the Wapping plant. (David Hoffman Photo Library)*

into a chair and the landlady brought a brandy and hurried off to call an ambulance. All this was going on while a yuppyish girl reporter questioned us about the strike and we gave our answers in whispers because of the rumours that all the local pubs were infiltrated by plain-clothes policemen. It all seemed very surreal.

I soon established a routine and would leave my car in Backchurch Lane, about a quarter of a mile from the plant, and walk to the clericals' meeting place at the junction of Dock Street and The Highway. The way to Dock Street was along narrow, cobbled streets between imposing Victorian warehouses. It was dark and almost deserted – except for the police. Sometimes I would pass a couple on foot patrol and look back to see them giving my car the once over. I often wondered about the wisdom of having the 'Murdoch is Bad News' sticker in the back window.

Next came the patrol car stationed at the top of Dock Street, where officers stopped vehicles attempting to enter their 'no go' area. Almost every week, someone would be trying to get in: there was a distressed chap who wanted to pick up his aged mother. She wasn't on the phone and he told them he couldn't let her know he wasn't able to reach the house. But they were unconcerned and, in the end, he had to drive away.

In Dock Street itself, one or two big green buses would be full of lounging policemen munching sandwiches, smoking and provocatively reading The Sun. *Further down, at the junction with The Highway, a cordon stretched right across the road. Sometimes they let you through and sometimes you were forced to take another route. There were more hospitable places to be on a Saturday night!*

The line of stoney-faced policemen closing off Thomas More Street, a favourite exit route for the TNT distribution lorries, would receive retaliatory taunts of 'overtime, overtime, overtime' and a large group of demonstrators would man the junction in case the convoy attempted to escape that way. The clerical members 'checked in' at Dock Street and either stayed to guard that point, or moved on to the main focus of the demonstration, which centered on the entrance to the Wapping plant on Virginia Street.

The News International complex, christened 'Fortress Wapping', was a deeply disturbing sight. Huge, square buildings were bathed in orange-yellow floodlights and surrounded by high spiked railings topped with coiled razor-wire. Two further coils of wire ran along the ground behind the railings and surveillance cameras peered over the top. Huge articulated lorries moved up a long concrete ramp and disappeared into the nearest building. All this was guarded by policemen standing four or five deep behind crash barriers placed across the top of Virginia Street, which lead down to the gate itself. And in the shadows behind, betrayed by the occasional tossing of a horse's head, or a glint of light on a shiny black helmet, the police on horseback waited.

A few hundred people stood about in The Highway and in Wellclose Street, which runs up a gentle slope to Wellclose Square. Here the unions had established a double-decker bus, mobile toilets and a tea van which, along with stalls selling cakes and strike memorabilia, grew into a veritable 'village' catering for the needs of the demonstrators. This area was considered 'safe' and the atmosphere, away from the 'front line' confronting the police in The Highway, was relaxed. It was unusual to see uniformed policemen here, although it was always assumed that there were plain clothes men in the crowd, and people were challenged by print-workers without being able to give satisfactory assurances about their identity. But, on occasions, there were uniformed officers present.

Denise: *I saw a young lad walking down Wellclose Street towards The Highway and as he passed a policeman in peaked cap and pips, he tripped on some discarded drinks cans. I don't know if a can hit the policeman, or if the clatter simply startled him, but he swung round as if under attack and told the boy to 'move on or you're nicked'. The lad showed some reluctance and was promptly arrested and frog-marched away. The incident brought a strident response from an elderly printer, who proceeded to harangue the officers who remained in the street: 'you should be ashamed of yourselves', he said over and over again. ' We didn't fight two world wars for people to be pushed around by kids like you.'*

As the strike continued, people became more familiar with the police and, as a result, contemptuous and less intimidated. They developed the courage to question their actions even though arrest, which before the dispute would have been unthinkable, was a constant possibility.

Denise: *I was with a small group of clerical strikers one night when we met some machine men. One of them was a* News of the World *Father of the Chapel. We were walking along The Highway, it was always free of traffic on Saturday nights because of the road blocks, talking together, when we were approached by a group of constables led by a short, fat, red-bearded Scottish Sergeant who ordered us onto the pavement. We went, followed by a stream of abuse from the belligerent little man. This was too much for the FOC, who turned on him demanding, 'have you finished?' and proceeded to give as good as he got, ridiculing him in front of his men. When an Inspector approached the scene, only the Sergeant fell silent.*

One particular weekday march to Wapping was escorted by large numbers of City of London Police and disrupted the busy afternoon traffic around Fleet Street and Ludgate Circus. We were discussing the remote possibility that the demonstration might, for once, prompt the evening news bulletins to carry a report, when an enraged Sergeant told us we were 'fucking taking the piss'. His outburst prompted one of the marchers to remind him of our right of peaceful protest, and we went on reminding him all the way to Wapping, which took about two hours.

Graham: *In contrast to the faceless men of the Met, there were some real characters among the City policemen. One Sergeant in particular stepped straight out of some Victorian melodrama. He was six feet four or five tall; his wide helmet straps had gaps on either side to accommodate his enormous ears, and buckled under the chin; he held brown leather gloves in his hand and smoothed a magnificent drooping moustache. My friend, who had lectured the other Sergeant, christened him McQuorqadale of the Yard.*

At Virginia Street, protestors vented their anger on any News International employees who ventured too near the perimeter fence and shouted 'scabs' as, under police escort, the convoys of lorries and workers' cars made their escape along Pennington Street. Regularly, at about midnight, the police cleared The Highway and restored the road to through traffic. They moved out in a long line from their station at the top of Virginia Street and surrounded the two or three hundred stalwarts who had stuck it out. Slowly but relentlessly, the net drew tighter and tighter, squeezing everyone back up into Wellclose Street. There was always someone who didn't move quickly enough, or took exception to being manhandled, and this ended in the inevitable arrest.

The concentration of the mass of demonstrators at the plant entrance meant the distribution lorries used a number of alternative routes among the maze of back streets surrounding the plant. So strikers tried to cover the other exits as best they could.

Graham: *Opposite Wapping Lane, the pavement along The Highway is elevated, with railings running along it. When I arrived with a couple of work-mates, the fence was lined with people and across the road a cordon of policemen closed off the top of the Lane. Nothing happened until the police standing in the road began moving casually onto the pavements. Then, suddenly, there was the sound of racing engines and a police car, with its headlights blazing, roared up Wapping Lane and swung right into The Highway, closely followed by three TNT lorries going like hell.*

The cry of 'scabs' went up and the first lorry swung out across The Highway to make the turn. The cab came within four of five feet of us and I could clearly see the driver and his mate inside. Then a brick whistled past my head and smacked into the windscreen. It cracked in several directions and someone ran off down an alley behind us. The convoy sped on and the policemen opposite ran headlong across The Highway and clambered over the railings, pushing and shoving and arresting the wrong man for throwing the brick, dragging him away while he and his companions vainly protested his innocence.

After the mêlée, two of us wandered east along The Highway to Glamis Road and came across a large group of young people wrecking street furniture and tearing up paving stones for ammunition. We were remonstrating with them when a resident of the high-rise block overlooking the junction came down and explained to them that people had to live in the place the rest of the week and that life would not be made any easier by vandalized streets. They were 16 or 17 years old, infuriatingly self-righteous, and they treated us to a patronizing political lecture. The poor resident went home shaking his head.

There were rarely enough demonstrators present to block all the available exits, which would have taken many thousands of people, and if one group was seen by police to be effectively blocking an escape route, van loads of officers were sent in to make sure the area was cleared.

Joyce: *I took some miners down to Wapping one Saturday night: the Hackney Print Workers Support Group had links with Oakfield Colliery in South Wales. They saw a copper down there who had worked at their pit and after the strike he had joined the Met! They said to me, 'how the hell do you picket a place like this?' There was usually one entrance at a pit. They looked at it and said, 'God Joyce, you've got no chance, the size of this bloody place.'*

Michele: *It was about three or four in the morning, at the top of Glamis Road. We were all standing around in the road and one of the guys had a walkie-talkie keeping us in touch with how the other pickets were doing. We were actually succeeding in blocking the exit and not one lorry had come out. There was an old sofa there and some of the girls were taking it in turns to sit down. There was only a handful of ordinary policemen there and the atmosphere was really calm. Then, all of a sudden, we heard this roar. I was standing with a handful of girls, the men and women seemed to have separated, and I could see all these white vans coming down the road. I heard the doors open and C said 'run!' So I ran. The riot police got out and chased us. I didn't know at the time where my husband was, but I learned afterwards that some of the men sat down in the road and the police just ran over and clobbered as many people as they could. L caught up with us and she was hysterical because she saw one of the older men go down. He must have been in his seventies and the police clubbed him. She bent over him to see if he was alright and kept screaming 'He's dead, he's dead' and one of the riot police told her to get out of it or he would clobber her as well. When we stopped running I was in a state of shock, I couldn't believe what had happened and I couldn't see my husband.*

John: *One night at Dock Street, when a guy got knocked over by a horse, I shouted out to the police, 'have you got him an ambulance?', and one of the mounted policemen lifted his visor and said, very politely and in an incredibly posh voice, 'oh yes, I believe we have'. I'd read in history books that the cavalry were always upper crust. We were on the pavement and they told us to get into the road. But we wouldn't go. We said, 'no, because you're going to charge us. We won't go'.*

Frank: *There was one occasion: I'd gone to Wapping on a Saturday evening; I got off the bus in Commercial Road and as I made my way along The Highway towards Wellclose Square, I had to go through the line of police to join the main body of demonstrators. One of the coppers very politely stood aside and let me through with a 'good evening sir' – typical 'Dixon of Dock Green'. Maybe it was because I didn't wear the casual gear. I didn't have any casual gear, so I always went down in my respectable office garb: suit, raincoat and what have you. He didn't realise I was one of the 'Ugly Mob' and I thought, 'what a hypocrite', you'll probably be charging me in a few minutes.*

They would reopen The Highway at 11.30pm and on one occasion, when we'd all been pushed off the road, there'd been a few fisticuffs. When it was all settled down and everyone was back behind the barriers, the police withdrew and made their way back to their old transit vans and one of them looked at me gloatingly and said, 'we won', and I thought, 'you bastard'.

SOGAT★NGA★AUEW★NUJ
NEWS INTERNATIONAL DISPUTE

SATURDAY DEMONSTRATIONS

EACH SATURDAY EVENING THERE WILL BE A MAJOR DEMONSTRATION AT WAPPING IN SUPPORT OF THE PRINTWORKERS DISMISSED BY

RUPERT MURDOCH.

STRIKE GRAPHICS

ALL TRADE UNIONISTS AND SUPPORTERS ARE ASKED TO GIVE MAXIMUM SUPPORT.

MARCHES BEGIN AT 8~30ᴾᴹ AT TOWER HILL
PLEASE BE THERE EVERY WEEK

Printed by Southwark TUSU, 42 Braganza Street, SE17

10

The Police

Despite the role played by the police at Warrington and during the Miners' Strike, many News International strikers were totally unprepared for what they were to experience during the course of their own dispute. Even though union activists had reported what they had seen during the dispute with Eddie Shah and in the coalfields, there still existed an element of scepticism that the police were capable of such actions. This defensive attitude towards the police was even more evident during the unrest in the inner cities in 1981 and 1985.

It didn't take long, however, for attitudes to change dramatically for, despite comments from senior police officers that they were the 'meat in the sandwich', their role quickly became obvious. They were deployed to see that Murdoch got his papers onto the streets, thereby ensuring the success of his Wapping operation and the breaking of the unions. It was a role initiated by a Government who saw the destruction of organized labour as one of its central policies.

On 22nd January 1986, before the talks between the company and the unions had broken down, the Commissioner of Police for the Metropolitan Area invoked legislation dating from 1839, which gave the police the power to restrict pedestrian and vehicular movement in Tower Hamlets, where the Wapping plant is situated. And on the afternoon of the 24th, before the dispute was officially announced, all vehicles were removed from the vicinity of the News International buildings in Gray's Inn Road and metal barriers erected around their perimeters.

Deputy Assistant Commissioner Wyn Jones was put in overall charge of police operations at Wapping. He had previously been in command of policing at the Greenham Common air base in Berkshire, where groups of women had set up peace camps to protest against the decision of the Government to allow cruise missiles to be based there.

The arrests, and consequent criminalization, of the strikers began at a very early stage of the dispute. On Saturday 1st February, with strikers still shocked that Murdoch was able to produce and distribute

◀ *Police mass before a charge on demonstrators at Wapping (3/5/86). (David Hoffman Photo Library)*

his papers and with picketing at a very disorganized stage, only 500 people turned up to demonstrate outside the Wapping plant. They were met by a corresponding number of policemen. As the delivery lorries prepared to leave, orders were given for the demonstrators to move out of the road and the police began pushing the pickets back. Anyone who showed any sign of resistance was pulled out of the crowd and led to a waiting police van. Sixteen people were arrested, thirteen charged with obstruction and three with assault, and strikers were shocked by their first encounters with the police. The clearing of the road, and the accompanying random arrests of pickets, were to become regular occurrences over the course of the following year.

During the early months of the strike, the police tactics appeared to be to arrest people on charges of obstruction, or for public order offences. Those arrested were usually bound over to keep the peace. The effect of this action was to discourage people from participating in the demonstrations for fear of re-arrest and some of the bind-overs carried an instruction that they should not go within one mile of the picket lines at Wapping.

The SOGAT solicitors actively encouraged people to accept a bind-over, which caused much anger, as most of the arrests were on a random basis and many people wished to contest the charges. However, the London Machine Branch adopted a policy of contesting them and, consequently, many of the charges were dropped, with the police offering no evidence when the cases came to court.

There was a great deal of dissatisfaction with the union lawyers, a feeling that they just wanted to get the cases out of the way as quickly as possible. One clerical member turned up at court to find that his solicitor had a copy of *The Times* tucked in his briefcase.

Many of those arrested began looking elsewhere for representation and, as the dispute progressed and arrests increased, other initiatives, such as the distributing of 'Rights Cards' to demonstrators began. The cards, emanating from the Haldane Society of Socialist Lawyers and the Tower Hamlets Trades Council, gave information about a person's legal rights when under arrest.

As the demonstrations grew larger at Wapping, so did the numbers of police. Three weeks into the strike, on Saturday 15th February, official figures showed that over 1,000 police were present in expectation of the biggest picket so far. Among this number were eight Special Patrol Group (SPG) sections with full riot gear.

Over 2,000 people took part in the march from Tower Hill to

Wapping and the police, consequently, had a much tougher time dispersing the crowd as the TNT lorries prepared to leave the plant. Suddenly a gap opened in the police lines and 20 officers on horseback drove into the demonstrators. As people scattered to avoid the charge, the Special Patrol Group rushed in with batons and shields. They appeared in a state of frenzy: shouting, screaming, swearing and lashing out at anybody within range.

Just as suddenly, they retreated, melting away behind the lines from whence they came and leaving demonstrators in a state of shock. For many, it was the first time they had seen the police behaving like hooligans and they were frightened and uncomprehending.

Based on the statistic that only six of the 65 people arrested on 15th February were print workers, the media went to great lengths to stress the role of what they called 'the extreme left' at the demonstrations. The leaders of the unions involved, and the Labour Movement in general, condemned the 'outsiders' and from the outset actively discouraged external support for the pickets.

At the start of the strike Tony Dubbins said 'we are in this dispute to get sympathy from the public' and that 'we have got to accept the TUC guidelines and recognize that public sympathy about this issue is all important. Clearly the public was not very enamoured by what went on during the miners' strike'. But within a very short time, the strikers realized they couldn't win the dispute by themselves and were calling for mass demonstration at Wapping.

During the day-to-day picketing at Gray's Inn Road, Bouverie Street and Wapping, there was soon very little dialogue at all with the police officers on duty. The events at Wapping on Saturday nights could not easily be forgotten on Sunday morning and, within a few weeks of the beginning of the dispute, an intense bitterness had grown up towards the Force. This dislike, sometimes bordering on hatred, was particularly aimed at the Met, whose 'patch' covered the Wapping plant, and some policemen became known as being particularly nasty individuals who enjoyed getting 'stuck in' to pickets when the opportunity arose.

A tactic developed by the strikers was divide and rule, something more usually utilized by the employer. This ploy was used in several different ways, with high-ranking officers being the targets: senior officers were regularly told, for instance, how much better they were than one of their colleagues and vice-versa. Spreading rumours about what one or other of the officers had said the previous week was also designed to create an atmosphere of distrust among them.

A further tactic was to try to isolate the Met by playing other forces off against them. The marches to Wapping began at Tower Hill, which was controlled by the City of London Police, and though demonstrators did not actually believe that they behaved any differently than the Met on the picket lines, time was spent deriding the Met in favour of the City. There were even strikers' songs which played one force against the other.

After any major incident at the plant the police would hold a news conference explaining how their officers had behaved impeccably and displaying an horrific array of weapons, which had allegedly been used by the pickets to attack them. A caretaker from a school near the plant found two policemen removing an iron spike railing which was set in concrete and formed part of the fencing around the school. He challenged them to stop but they ignored him. That evening he was watching the television news and saw the railing produced by the police who claimed it was thrown at them by demonstrators.

Ordinary people, who a few weeks earlier had been librarians, cashiers, cleaners and printers were, as part of the propaganda exercise waged against the strikers, branded as thugs and described as if they were part of some sinister underground movement.

Pam: *My attitude towards the police began to change during the Miners' Dispute. Until then I always thought they were marvellous. But my perception hardened considerably during our own strike. Now I can't even talk to my Bobby at home who's a very peaceful 'Plod' type. I feel very hostile towards them all and I don't like feeling that way. I think a lot of it was their orders: they were told how to be. They stopped being human, they were a machine.*

Helen: *The police? I hate them. Towards the end of the strike, my dad and I were going to the fish and chip shop near home when we saw an accident and went to help. The driver was pretty shaken and I told her I'd find a policeman. I found one and was trying to help when he said 'I know you don't I?' My dad looked at me as if to say 'what have you done?' 'You go to Wapping' the policeman said, 'you and your mates go down there and take the piss out of us. Well, you're marked lovie, you're marked'. 'Oh my God' I thought.*

When I saw what they did to the miners, I thought maybe they were provoked, but I was called a 'C U Next Tuesday', an old slag, a bastard. What kind of person talks to a girl like that? The police do. If I ever got mugged or worse, raped, I don't know what I'd do. I honestly don't think I could turn to a policeman or woman.

Pickets became very wary of police infiltrators. Much of the time on the picket line was spent discussing the strike and it was easy to mingle with the crowd and pick up snippets of information. People became suspicious of any unfamiliar face and it was common to see pickets checking the identity of a stranger. They knew that they were being videotaped by the police because it had been confirmed in Parliament by the Home Secretary, and there was a strong suspicion that microphone surveillance was being operated from surrounding buildings, although this was never proven.

Only one 'grass' was uncovered during the strike: A SOGAT member (working in newspaper distribution) who acted as a steward on many demonstrations, was thought to have been singled out by the police, who identified him as a weak link because of his willingness to obey their instructions. Whenever problems arose during a march, it was noticeable that he was constantly telling the marchers what the police wanted them to do and suggesting they agree to it. This behaviour caused a great deal of annoyance but, because of his acknowledged commitment to the strike, a quiet word was considered sufficient admonishment. He had also been involved in flying picket activities and during one of these sorties he was arrested. Perhaps the police had suggested, then, that he furnish them with information in return for dropping the charges against him.

Eventually, events began to be anticipated by the police (fuelling suspicions that there was an informer among the strikers) and a trap was laid. In the same way that false information was given out on the telephone, to prove that they were being tapped, spurious plans were fed to the spy and, as suspected, the police turned up for an event that never was. The informant immediately disappeared from the strike and left his job in the industry soon afterwards.

The police continually taunted the strikers, waving their overtime forms and copies of *The Sun* at every opportunity. This made people very angry, but more resilient. In return, the police were taunted with chants of 'Paper Boys' for their role in helping to get Murdoch's papers delivered. The strikers also realized that just being at Wapping during the long, cold days and nights when nothing happened was draining police morale, despite the extra money in their pockets.

Despite Government denials that the dispute was affecting policing in other areas of London, it was clear that police resources were being stretched. The police journal, *The Job*, carried many statements by senior officers showing that crime levels were increasing due to lack of available officers. By January 1987, 1.2 million police hours had been worked in connection with the dispute and it was estimated that policing costs were £5.5 million. The strikers' newspaper, *The Wapping Post*, obtained the pay slips of two officers working at Wapping which showed the take-home pay of a constable to be £1,183 in September 1986 and £1,463 in October, an average of £300 a week.

11

The Ops Room

The clerical strikers made many valuable contributions to the dispute, but one of the most vital, perhaps, was the setting up and running of the strike headquarters. Known as the Operations Room, or Ops Room, it was situated on the top floor of the Clerical Branch offices at Caxton House near the Elephant and Castle, and its function was to give and receive information and advice, twenty-four hours a day, seven days a week.

The Ops Room came into being the day after the strike began and was run, initially, by clerical chapel officials who spent the first couple of days telephoning activists in an effort to galvanize support for the initial picketing of the TNL and NGN buildings.

Rotas were then drawn up for its staffing by members, which were organized on a three shift basis, with three people on each day shift and two on all-night sessions. The phones rang non-stop: there were requests for speakers to address meetings all over the country and for literature and posters for distribution at workplaces and union branches. There were calls from strikers seeking welfare advice and information on the progress of the strike and brave souls recounting tales of derring-do (e.g. stealing bundles of *The Sun* from the pavement outside their local newsagent's shop). It also became the place to pop into when you felt isolated and needed reassurance. All the strike gossip and rumours filtered their way through the Ops Room.

One or two activities were somewhat bizarre: for a couple of weeks, for instance, all the registration numbers of the TNT lorries used at Wapping were noted and strikers followed them in cars to find out their destinations. All the information gathered was passed on to the Ops Room but, given that a copy of the firm's annual report would have shown exactly where their depots were situated, it seems, in hindsight, to have been a terrible waste of time.

It was widely believed that both telephones in the Ops Room were bugged and to test this theory, misinformation was given out about the whereabouts of pickets. Strikers then went to the places where the spurious action was supposed to be taking place and found them swarming with police. Subsequently, great care was taken over what was said on the telephone.

Lots of people did sterling work in the Ops Room throughout the year-long strike but two, by virtue of their commitment and their old-fashioned values, not to mention an ability to talk the hind legs off a donkey, stood apart. Renee Hussey was the provider of a constant supply of sandwiches and beans on toast to those on duty. Always immaculately dressed and coiffured and dripping with jewellery, Renee was a model of enthusiasm and never even contemplated defeat. With 29 years' service on *The News of the World* behind her, she was offered £28,000 by Murdoch to quit the dispute. 'How dare he insult me', she said.

Frank Jordan, urbane in suit, tie and gabardine raincoat, staffed the phones on the big Wapping demo nights and if you were after an informed opinion, articulately expressed, Frank was your man.

Frank: *I got a phone call saying they wanted people for the Ops Room, would I be prepared to come and man the phones and so on. I said "Yes", and very soon you got little groups of people doing the same shifts on a more or less regular basis. My main nights were Wednesday and Saturday, the big demo nights, so when I was on duty it was a bit lively down at Wapping. There were a lot of arrests and you felt you were in the nerve-centre. On the other hand, you missed out on the banter on the picket line. In my job, I usually dealt with the other managers, I didn't know the staff, but I got to know people during the strike and I felt a tremendous bond of friendship which, to me, is one of the great things to come out of all this.*

People found a new sense of purpose. I lost a job I loved, but at the same time I was very committed to the dispute. Sometimes I thought, 'hell, what have I done. I've given up my job and I'll never get another one like it'. But it was something I couldn't turn my back on because of my basic belief in what I saw as a democratic right to strike and not be sacked, a right which was taken away from us. I just had to fight it.

On Saturday nights, the largest crowds gathered at Wapping and police activity was at its highest. Inevitably, there were arrests. Details of these were relayed from the picket lines to the Ops Room, where efforts were made to find out where the detainees had been taken. Then the lawyers were contacted so they would have legal representation. Information about arrests and injuries was then passed onto the picket's families. It was an anxious enough time for those left at home on a Saturday night and, though the news itself was traumatic, it was very important that people should know why their loved one hadn't come home.

As the dispute went through peaks and troughs, so did the activity in the Ops Room and, early in July, the evening shifts (except for those on Wednesdays and Saturdays, when the larger demonstrations at Wapping took place) were discontinued by the branch committee as part of a cost-cutting exercise. Despite the fact that the dispute was going through a flat period, the decision angered the clerical strikers who saw it as another step away from the total commitment they demanded from their representatives.

During these times of low activity the Ops Room, like the picket lines, became a place for endless debate. The talking was a safety valve, fulfilling a constant need to communicate with others in the same boat. It was also a continuing search for something hopeful in a situation that often seemed hopeless. The Ops Room was the clerical heartland.

Pam: *I knew I didn't have what it takes to stand on a picket line going off at people, as bad as I felt inside, so I thought, 'best thing I can do is something more constructive'. I enjoyed it in the Ops Room. During the first few months things were happening all the time and I felt at the hub of things. Before I went up there I used to feel sick at home, worrying all the time and feeling so dreadfully cut off. Up there you felt you were a part of what was going on. You started at a very uncivilized hour in the morning, but it became a way of life.*

During the bitterly cold early weeks of the strike, the pickets at Bouverie Street, Grays Inn Road, Wapping and elsewhere needed to be sustained and, to this end , hundreds of bread rolls were delivered each morning to Caxton House, where they were buttered and filled with ham and cheese by a battery of clerical strikers. These rolls, along with a large tea urn and plenty of tea and sugar, were loaded into the back of an old and none too reliable transit van and driven to the various picket lines. It was noted that relationships with previously patronizing Machine Branch strikers began to show a marked improvement.

The van went to Wapping every day and, almost every day, as it turned off The Highway to go down to the six pickets at the main entrance, the demonstrators in Wellclose Square, not realising its purpose, dished out the same verbal onslaught and finger pointing received by every other vehicle approaching the plant. It happened despite the fact that, on its way back from the main gate, it would often stop in the Square to distribute any surplus tea and rolls!

When the transit was out of action, as it often was, a tiny Metro was employed and, due to the lack of space inside, spillages were common. Its cloth seats were much more difficult to clean than the transit's metal floor and, after a while, the stench was so unbearable that, even on the coldest days, the car travelled with all its windows open.

Helen: Maxine and I started going to all of the meetings when the strike started. We got to know the activists in our chapel. We couldn't help getting caught up in it ourselves, but I suppose we first got involved because Maxine was learning to drive. We volunteered to do the tea runs to the pickets in Gray's Inn Road, Bouverie Street and Wapping because it meant Maxine could drive the SOGAT Metro. That's how it all started! We enjoyed it, having a chat with all the different pickets. It was a great way to get to know people and they were always glad to see us, especially in the middle of the night.

After the first few days of dealing with the roll mountain, the clerical team expressed a unanimous and heartfelt wish never to see another roll and, not too many weeks later, even the previously grateful pickets were heard to murmur the same sentiment.

There were many different levels of commitment to the strike. Many people lived it day and night while others, people who had found new jobs for instance, didn't participate at all. But it was important to distinguish between those who were just inactive and those who were actually scabbing. When the non-participants were identified, every effort was made to encourage them to play some kind of role, no matter how small.

Following a check of the membership, only one person remained unaccounted for and he, along with all the known scabs, was sent a letter by the branch secretary asking him to appear before the branch committee to explain his actions. On 7th May, over three months after the dispute began, he turned up at the branch, clutching his letter.

John: I was in the Ops Room when I got a call from reception telling me that someone wanted to see me. I was stunned when I saw Monty. To be honest, I'd forgotten all about him. With everything that was going on, it was very easy to forget people you hadn't seen since the dispute started, but I shouldn't have forgotten Monty because I had been involved, with another shop steward, in negotiating a proper job description and pay rise for him. He was in his mid-fifties, lived alone and kept himself to himself. He was very quiet but, once you got to know him, very friendly. He never complained about anything and the journalists on the subs floor where he worked took full advantage of his good nature. He was so grateful when we were able to sort out his job description for him that he took us both out to lunch.

Standing in reception in his old overcoat and carrying his plastic shopping bags, he made a forlorn figure. He was visibly upset and the first thing he said was, 'I'm not a scab'. I asked him where he'd been and why he hadn't collected his strike pay and he said, 'I've just been sitting at home, or wandering the streets. I didn't want to be a burden to anyone, but my savings have run out'. He hadn't signed on as unemployed and only turned up at the branch because he received the letter sent to the scabs. One thing was certain, Monty had not crossed the picket line.

There was only one thing to do and that was to get him involved. I spent a couple of hours chatting to him and showing him around the Ops Room. With his Unemployment Benefit sorted out and his position explained to the branch secretary, he was soon working, almost full time, on the Wapping Post.

The other strikers showed no animosity towards him and there was a general feeling of, 'well, better late than never'. He was certainly better off being among friends, knowing what was going on and being a part of it. He was the only one who slipped through the net.

WANTED: THE DIRTY RIPPER

12

Speaking

Once the dispute started, requests for speakers to attend meetings around the country began to be received. Members of the clerical chapels were in great demand as they represented a section of the workforce that people did not generally associate with the printing industry.

Tim: *I was sitting at home, seeing how many coins I could spin at once on the coffee table and I thought 'this is ridiculous, I'm fighting for my job!' So I went down to Caxton House and asked what I could do. Although I didn't feel qualified to speak at meetings, I replaced the assistant branch secretary at a meeting in Oxford and realized I could do it.*

Deirdre: *I have to say that I really enjoyed the speaking engagements, although I was absolutely terrified at first. I'm not shy, but for the first time I felt the onus was really on me to prove our case. I spent a lot of time the night before writing and re-writing my speech but, in the end, I didn't really use it. After that I didn't bother to write anything down. It got to the point where if I saw a microphone, I wanted to leap up and make a speech. I remember going to a dance, at a golf club or somewhere, and there was a microphone and I really wanted to get up there and collect some money.*

It was harder speaking to the chapel, proposing motions and convincing people to support them. Many members were older than me, but they started asking me for advice. I think that was the hardest thing of all. You don't mind helping people, or listening to their problems, but I found out that it is easy to sway people and that was a great responsibility. I was lucky, my husband was working, so we weren't suffering the financial hardship that a lot of others were. I couldn't go to a chapel meeting and look them in the eye and tell them it was going to be alright. That wore me out in the end. That finished me off.

Graham: *I live in a conservative, semi-rural area in Hertfordshire. The local Labour Parliamentary candidate lives a few doors away from me and when we met in the street during the strike, he would ask me how things were going. We tended to expect people to be better informed about the dispute than they appeared to be, which was probably a bit unrealistic, but for someone in his position he seemed to know very little about it. I lamented the lack of solid support from the Labour Party and he indicated that they were distancing themselves from unpopular causes! But he asked me if I would speak at a couple of local Party meetings. I'd made one or two brief contributions to debates at chapel meetings and had done a television interview on the union bus at Wapping for a BBC programme, but standing up and making a speech in front of a group of total strangers was something else. Anyway, I said I would do it.*

It was very cold on the night of the first meeting, which was held in the Community Hall of a neighbouring village. The ten minute drive didn't allow the heater in my car time to do its work and when we arrived, it was colder inside the hall than it was outside. I was introduced to the Chairman, who invited me to sit next to him facing the five or six stalwarts who had showed up. Even so, I was nervous. I'd prepared some notes beforehand and began tentatively: 'I was a Librarian at The Times *and I'm a member of the SOGAT clerical chapel, which has a membership of about 500. We are secretaries, storemen, telephonists and clerks. I'm sure you are aware of the background to the dispute (actually I had my doubts), so I thought I'd just say a few words about how you can help'. I went on to explain the role of the EETPU in the affair and asked them to demand that the TUC instruct the electricians to stop doing our jobs. I asked them not to buy Murdoch's papers and to persuade others to do the same; to distribute the handbills I had brought with me and to make regular donations to our hardship fund, explaining that any strike pay we received depended entirely on contributions from people like themselves. I finished by saying that perhaps the most important thing they could do would be to go down to Wapping on a Saturday night and see what was happening for themselves.*

The Chairman invited questions from the floor and these came steadily for an hour. The questioners, especially the lady who knitted throughout the meeting and stopped only to ask her question, expressed a great deal of concern for the plight of the strikers. I did my best, but found it more and more difficult to stop my teeth from chattering long enough to answer the questions coherently. I was very relieved when someone suggested a donation and was able to leave them discussing 'a small contribution' to the strike fund.

The second meeting was more daunting. It took place at the Constituency Labour Party headquarters, with the members seated around a group of tables pushed together in the middle of the room. The atmosphere was business-like. I made a similar speech to the one I made at the village hall, but the questioning this time betrayed a certain hostility. 'What about the violence?' 'How do you justify the over-inflated wages?' 'I am a teacher and we rely on The Times Educational Supplement *for jobs'. I was motivated by their attitude and needed a drink to keep my mouth from going dry.*

My Labour Party candidate didn't take up my offer to join me at Wapping and I doubt if any of them took the trouble to see for themselves.

I only addressed one more meeting outside the chapel: the local Young Socialists. I was invited by a lad in my village who had asked for a lift to Wapping after seeing the strike poster in my front window. He went to the demonstrations regularly until he was arrested for assault, trying to pull a friend from the clutches of the police. I don't know anyone less likely to commit assault than him and with the help of a character reference from our local candidate, who was a magistrate, he was bound over. When I told the candidate that the Young Socialists had asked me to address their meeting, he shook his head and said they were 'Militant'.

The chair-person, an eloquent and earnest young woman of about 17, conducted the meeting impeccably, with most of the telling contributions coming from her punk friend, who was the only other girl present. The four boys, who included my friend, were more reticent. They brought some badges and we went off to the bar where the discussion centred on the merits of Red Wedge and Billy Bragg and the girl who had chaired the meeting told me how her friend had been arrested while they picketed South Africa House and was sexually assaulted in the back of the police van.

Carmel: *When the dispute began I had to learn to speak in front of all kinds of audiences – before I had just spoken briefly as a committee member at chapel meetings.*

To begin with, I was very nervous. My legs shook so much I thought I'd fall over. What helped me was knowing, from my previous experience of chapel meetings, that most people in the audience would be scared to stand up and speak too. At my first meeting, which was at IPC magazines in Sutton, I was speaking to a chapel rather like ours. I began by describing the Wapping plant, the methods of picketing and incidents that were occurring, and then asked for questions. A large burly man stood up. 'My brother knows a man who works with you lot and he earns a fortune and hardly ever goes to work,' he said. 'Why should we support you?'

Taken aback, I replied that I had earned a take home salary of £146 a week. 'You should come and work down here,' he jeered. I leaned forward and said in a menacing tone, 'Do you object to women earning £146 a week?' The audience, the majority of whom were women, were amused. We carried the day and they took a collection for us.

It was at a meeting on International Women's Day (8th March) that I made a kind of breakthrough as regards public speaking and out of sheer anger, I spoke better than I had ever done before. I had been invited to speak at a rally at Fulham Town Hall along with the MPs Joan Ruddock and Clare Short and Glenys Kinnock (the wife of the Labour Party leader, Neil Kinnock).

I arrived a bit late from the Wapping picket line with Deirdre and it seemed that having missed our turn, we would not get a chance to speak at all. I listened to speeches about women's struggle, both in Britain and the Third World, poems about women, and then a concluding speech by Glenys Kinnock, followed by the chair's announcement that there would be wine, food and dancing.

I got to my feet. 'Just one minute,' I said to a startled audience. 'It's International Women's Day and I've just left thousands of wonderful women marching on Fortress Wapping because I was under the misapprehension that I'd been invited to speak here tonight'.

I strode to the front of the meeting. 'I'll only take two minutes of your time'. Taking a deep breath I blanked out my embarrassment and opened up. 'I've listened with interest to the previous speakers, I've been a victim of the things that they spoke of including poor housing and being a single parent and once again I find myself a victim ... a victim of vicious anti-trades union legislation brought in by the Tories and used by press barons like Rupert Murdoch ...'

I spoke for about 3 minutes, telling them about the women's role in the dispute and invited them to visit us on the picket line. The words had come out of a black hole and I was aware of watching them spill into the audience. I finished and walked towards the back of the hall. I was in a state of trance. At first the audience seemed stunned; then they clapped, cheered and stamped their feet. I was kissed by several people before I got to the back of the hall. 'You shamed them' someone shouted. Later Glenys Kinnock came up and said 'it was a most effective speech'.

Later on that month, I went to Glamorgan with Deirdre to three mining villages which her father's chapel had adopted during the miners' strike. The women there specially asked for women speakers as guests to mark the anniversary of their own strike.

The community consisted of the three villages along a valley with the Seven Sisters Pit, set in bleak countryside with rounded hills, quite pretty in parts. There were about 700-800 houses in each village. In the one where we stayed, everyone was part of the mining community and they had only one scab during the whole dispute.

The women in that area had come into their own during their strike. They picked us up in a bright red van which they referred to as 'our gay van'. I thought they meant that it was brightly coloured, but I discovered the reason was that it had been a present from the Lesbian and Gay Support Group in London. The women absolutely loved having their own van and they whipped up and down their valleys in it during and after the dispute.

On the night that we spoke they fed 1,000 people at their centre and the money raised went to us and to other groups of workers who were in dispute at that time. We got £250 each. This was the first time that I had to speak through a microphone to so many people. I can't speak with a bit of paper in my hand, I just take a deep breath, breathe out and then speak straight from the heart.

That particular night I met Terry Thomas, Vice President of the South Wales miners and he invited me to do a week's tour of his area, speaking to miners, which I did in June. I did three pit meetings a day, the first at 5.45am, the second at 12.30pm and the third at 9.45pm. I also did Labour Party and other union meetings, in all between 5 to 7 meetings per day. During that month, I had about 4 hours sleep a night and I lost a stone in weight.

I went into the first meetings to wolf whistles. The miners were quite shocked to have a SOGAT speaker who wasn't a big burly printer. I usually tried to relax them by saying 'you're obviously very surprised to see a female printer. Well let me tell you that, like you, I'm a shift worker and I'm used to working with a lot of hard heavy men-printers'. That would usually produce a laugh and they would settle down and start to listen.

Most of the meetings were held in the canteen, although occasionally a very belligerent manager would prevent this and I would have to address the meeting outside by shouting above the noise of a lot of machinery. I usually had about 12 minutes to speak and I assured them that I hadn't come begging for their money because I knew that they were still financially embarrassed. I told them that I wanted their co-operation in making sure that the scab papers weren't sold anywhere in their valleys and that, if they could come, I would like to see them at Wapping now and then. That was what I was after and that was what they gave us.

Tim*: I spoke at a teachers' rally in Edinburgh with a chap from the Glasgow Southside Support Group. But he missed the coach back and I was left holding the baby: £1300 in cash in two buckets. Staggering out of the bus station back in Glasgow, I found myself on Sauchiehall Street in the middle of the rush-hour: conspicuous, vulnerable and completely at a loss how to conceal the money. But I got a cab, made it back to the hotel and struggled up several flights of stairs, my arms now two inches longer than when I started, to the room. The maid burst in while I was counting the money and demanded a 'cut' to keep her mouth shut. Sometimes there seems no point in trying to explain.*

EAST ENDERS RECLAIM OUR STREETS FROM MURDOCHS BOOTBOYS

13

Residents

The clerical chapel's first attempt at contact with the Wapping residents was not entirely successful. A week after the dispute started, as part of a public relations exercise, three strikers visited the tower blocks opposite the News International plant: at two o'clock in the afternoon, there was a strange silence throughout the flats. Hardly anybody would open their front doors and those who did had to undo a whole array of security devises. They explained that many elderly people in the blocks felt very vulnerable, only venturing out when absolutely necessary. They would not open their doors if they didn't recognize a caller through the spy hole.

When the strikers asked residents to sign a petition protesting against the noise made by the TNT lorries leaving the plant late at night, they were happy to oblige. Unexpectedly, however, they stressed that the racket made by the pickets shouting *at* the lorries was the greater problem. As the dispute progressed, however, many residents became firm supporters of the strike. When a clerical striker was invited to address a meeting of the Stephen and Matilda House Co-operative in Thomas More Street, close to the News International plant, there was tremendous enthusiasm for the dispute and residents offered over-night accommodation to those pickets and demonstrators who experienced difficulties getting home.

The police made their own attempts to win over Wapping residents: Tenants Association meetings were targeted in an effort to justify road blocks and other restrictions on residents' freedom of movement and, in early March, they organized their own meeting for residents. The few people who turned up were met by strikers handing out leaflets which apologized for the inconvenience caused by the picketing and demonstrations and putting the print workers' side in the dispute with News International.

Tower Hamlets Trades Council produced and distributed leaflets to the large local Bangladeshi community, calling for their support for the strikers and a boycott of the newspapers produced at Wapping. But this was the only serious initiative and links between the strikers

◀ *Residents demonstrate at Wapping against Murdoch and the police (24/1/87).*
(David Hoffman Photo Library)

and the local Bangladeshis never materialized. This was a great pity, as it may have helped to break down many of the prejudices that existed within the predominantly white London print industry and could have helped to raise awareness of the attacks by groups of fascists who were active in the area.

On 27th February 1986, the National Council for Civil Liberties (NCCL) initiated an investigation into the policing strategy in Wapping and how it was affecting local residents. The decision was made after the NCCL had received a number of complaints from local people alleging their freedom of movement had been restricted since the beginning of the News International dispute.

The NCCL found that the police had regularly set up road blocks across a wide area of Wapping up to a mile from the News International plant, particularly on Saturday nights. These had effectively closed off the area so that entrance by car was almost impossible, with just one entrance, from Tower Bridge, having been left open. Residents in motor vehicles and on foot had been stopped at road blocks many times. People were asked to give their name and address, proof of identity, where they were going and why. Some had been accompanied to their door to check that they had given correct information.

Three women testified that, between them, they had been stopped 38 times since the dispute started. On one occasion they were going home with a male friend and were stopped by three policemen who asked where they were going and tried to turn them back. Ultimately, one of them showed her driving licence and log book and they were allowed to proceed. They claimed that the police were extremely rude and attempted to start trouble with the young man. They were deeply angered by the incident.

A 14-year-old girl was stopped at 9.30pm on a Saturday evening in late February. The police refused to let her cross The Highway to go down Wapping Lane and suggested she walk home across some wasteland. She told them her age and that it would be dangerous and insisted she take the direct route along The Highway. A nearby group of pickets pushed the police aside, allowing her to go on her way.

A young mother, with two children and a baby, was stopped while going home in a minicab on an extremely cold night. The driver was going down Thomas More Street, but the police refused to let him pass. The woman had to walk the rest of the way home along a dark street with her children. She said, 'the weather was really cold with ice and snow'.

A statement was taken from a Bethnal Green GP who had driven to Wapping to visit a patient. He left Prusom Street at 10.15pm, but found he could not drive into Wapping Lane. He took another route up Garnet Street and was stopped by police at the junction of Garnet Street and The Highway. He said the attitude of the police was 'dismissive', despite the fact that he explained who he was, and the purpose of his journey. The Highway was empty of people at that point. He finally managed to drive out of Wapping along Glamis Road. He said he found the situation 'horrific' and was very angry about what happened. 'If I am asked to visit again, I will say no' he said.

Some residents were arrested when refusing to give their identities or answer questions. One man, a resident of Vaughan Way, was arrested but not charged. At 11.30pm on Saturday 22nd March, he was walking home from Cable Street with two friends and was not allowed to go through the police barrier at the top of Wapping Lane, at its junction with The Highway. Continuing along The Highway, he was stopped again, this time at the barrier at the top of the footpath into Wapping Woods and asked by police officers for his name and address, which he gave, but refused to produce any proof of identification. Then, he alleges, he was pushed and sworn at by two officers and they said, 'nick him'. He was taken to a police bus parked in Garnet Street.

In the bus, he asked what he was being charged with and was told 'threatening behaviour'. He told them this was rubbish, being careful to argue as calmly as possible. Then, he alleges, the policeman said he would be charged with assault instead. During the time he was in the police bus, the four policemen would not tell him their names or which station they were from and that they were laughing and joking about the fact that they were on double time.

The resident was 'shoved unceremoniously' into Southwark Police Station, where he was interviewed by a Sergeant. With him were the officer who had sworn at him and the officer who had arrested him. They were, he alleged, fabricating a story about the arrest and the Sergeant was looking dubious. The man insisted that the officers were lying.

Afterwards, he was put in a cell for two hours, during which time another officer interviewed him and he noticed that his file contained a Polaroid photograph which had been taken during the earlier interview. He was told later that he was free to go and was not charged. On the night of his arrest he had been wearing a 'Wapping Resident' sticker and a badge supporting the print workers.

The NCCL found that the police gave priority to ensuring the passage of News International lorries, rather than protecting the rights and safety of residents. They received complaints about the noise and about the speed at which the lorries travelled around the side streets near the plant. A couple living in Welsh House, Wapping Lane, with their three children, said their lives had been made intolerable by the noise of the lorries going past their ground floor bedroom. They had given up going to bed until 2am on Saturday nights, when the lorries stopped. Another resident described the first time she heard the lorries as 'an earthquake'. A 30mph speed limit operates around the back streets of Wapping and all the residents interviewed said they were certain the lorries were travelling much, much faster. Some said they thought they went as fast as 60mph.

There had been a lorry ban imposed by the Greater London Council since 31st January 1986, which required lorries over 16 tons to display a plate at the rear and a permit disc on the windscreen, if they were travelling through London between 9pm and 7am and had been exempted from the ban. The NCCL observed that no News International vehicles, which were over the weight limit, displayed GLC exemption permits.

One Garnet Street resident complained that, on occasions, the pelican crossing on The Highway at the junction with Garnet Street had been switched off, she assumed to let the lorries through without delay. She felt very angry about this as The Highway is a fast, dangerous road and the residents had fought hard to get the crossing in the first place.

A Matilda House resident said that one evening, in late January, he was starting to cross the newly installed crossing at the junction of Dock Street, The Highway and East Smithfield. 'As I reached the crossing', he said, 'a lorry was coming from the east. Someone pressed the pelican button and the lights changed to red before the lorry reached them. But it drove right through. Luckily, I hadn't started to cross. The police then ran across the road towards some printers who were standing on the north side of The Highway, and yelled that they were committing an offence by pressing the button. There was a heated exchange as the printers took the officers' numbers and pointed out that they had let the lorry drive through a red light. The police eventually withdrew, saying they had seen no red light'.

A number of residents complained that bus services were being restricted, which added to their feelings of isolation. London Regional Transport confirmed that there had been a number of specific instances when the 22A route was terminated at Aldgate on a Friday or Saturday night, instead of continuing to Wapping, and that it had also happened on occasions during the week. The spokesman said that the buses stopped at Aldgate if they were told in advance by the police that there would be roadblocks in Wapping.

Pubs, clubs, restaurants and taxi firms reported considerable loss of earnings due to the virtual sealing off of the area and there were fears of long term loss of trade.

Throughout the dispute residents held regular marches and demonstrations to protest about the restrictions on their movements and the use of their streets to ensure the passage of News International's vehicles. This led to them facing the same treatment from the police as the strikers received and many ended up being arrested.

14

Murdoch's First Offer

Within a few weeks of the dispute starting, SOGAT were issued with a sequestration order by the courts for refusing to lift an instruction to its members in the wholesale distribution sector which told them not to handle News International's publications. The union's assets, worth around £17 million, were frozen and a fine of £25,000 imposed. The order allowed News International to select which firm they wanted to administer the union's funds and, consequently, chartered accountants Ernst and Whinney took control of all bank accounts, buildings and other assets, including the sick and benevolent funds. Two days after the sequestration order was issued, News International obtained another High Court injunction against the postal workers union ordering it to withdraw an instruction to its members to stop handling cards printed by *The Sun* for its daily bingo game.

For the first few weeks of the dispute, the clerical strikers had received strike pay of between £30 and £40 per week, but the sequestration order on the 10th February meant no strike pay was available that week. The uncertainty regarding money tested the resolve of the strikers but, on 24th March, a test case brought by the unions led to unemployment benefit of £30.45p per week becoming available to all those sacked by News International who were still out of work. The adjudication from the Department of Employment decided that, for benefit purposes, the strike had ended on 27th January when Murdoch had moved to Wapping.

A few days later, on Friday 28th March, *The Sun* and *The Times* were printed at Wapping. It was Good Friday and the longstanding tradition of the national newspapers not printing on that day had been broken.

On Friday 4th April, Murdoch made his first offer to settle the dispute: the announcement went out on the Channel 4 evening news programme and the details took the strikers by surprise. They were aware that News International had met with the arbitration service, ACAS, in the middle of February, but there had been minimal feedback on what had happened. They were also aware that the unions had met with representatives of the company twice in mid-March, through the auspices of the TUC. These meetings were ostensibly to try to open negotiations which, at that time, News International seemed reluctant to do.

However, the strikers were not aware that on the 22nd March, Brenda Dean had secretly met Murdoch at his home in Beverly Hills. In her autobiography, Dean tells how the one to one meeting with Murdoch took place by his swimming pool 'in the warmth of the Californian sun' and how Murdoch 'barbecued lamb chops' for the pair of them. She describes how her 'bottom line' was to obtain financial compensation for those sacked and how 'as we talked it through, so we got to know each other better. I have to say I liked him'. She continues: 'printing ink is clearly in his blood' and 'all he wanted to do was produce newspapers'. On the same evening at another meeting, this time in a restaurant, she states that 'by the end of the meal we had virtually agreed the dispute had to come to an end' and 'yes, there would be compensation for those of my members who had lost their jobs if and when I could find a way to force the final confrontation by my colleagues of the Wapping issue'.

And so, only 8 weeks after approximately 4,000 of her members had been sacked, the General Secretary of SOGAT, who appeared to be completely enamoured with the person who had thrown them on the scrapheap, had decided to end the dispute.

The offer came at a time when the numbers on the demonstrations at Wapping had been increasing. Following the first few weeks of the dispute, and the realization that a boycott campaign alone was not going to force the issue, the number of people attending the Saturday evening demonstrations began to grow and achieved some success in delaying the departure of the delivery lorries from the plant.

On 8th February a Women's March, led by Brenda Dean, attracted around 2,000 people and a similar number attended on the following week when, as previously mentioned, mounted police were deployed and 65 people were arrested. On 8th March, in celebration of International Women's Day, around 5,000 women led the Saturday evening demonstration from Tower Hill to Wapping and on the following Saturday, after a call from the strikers for a mass picket, around 7,000 people converged on the plant. Demonstrators began to dismantle the fencing at the front of the plant and riot police and mounted officers charged the crowd on several occasions. Twenty-six demonstrators were arrested and charged with public order offences.

In return for ending the dispute, Murdoch proposed giving the Times Newspapers building in Gray's Inn Road to the unions to produce a newspaper for the Labour Movement. This was the older of the two buildings and included 60 of the 90 printing presses. Brenda Dean was interviewed and stated that the offer could not form the whole of an agreement. Murdoch set a deadline of 7th May for a settlement to be reached.

Only the clerical branch committee was willing to look at the Gray's Inn Road offer, but the clerical strikers rejected the request to be involved in a feasibility study, being firmly of the opinion that it did not address the issue of union recognition at Wapping. They did not want to 'own' a newspaper where there would be a minimal number of jobs and Murdoch and some of the other proprietors would ensure that it was put out of business in a very short period of time.

The national union had employed Frank Barlow, a *Financial Times* executive, to carry out a feasibility study of the offer. Three months later, he announced that 400 jobs were to be lost at the *Financial Times*.

The Gray's Inn Road offer heralded a period of frantic activity. On Sunday 6th April, the first national rally of the dispute took place and, despite torrential rain, around 15,000 people gathered in Trafalgar Square. At times, especially during the harsh winter nights on the picket lines, the strikers had felt isolated and they were boosted by the sight of delegations from many different parts of the country.

On the same day, Murdoch placed adverts in *The Sunday Mirror* and *The People* criticizing the strikers for lost production over the past 10 years due to disputes, over-manning and inflated wage demands. There was surprise amongst many at the rally that printers at the two newspapers concerned had made no effort to prevent these attacks against their fellow union members appearing.

From the platform in the Square, trade union leaders and MPs expressed their solidarity with the strikers, but some contributions were greeted with cynicism and derision. To the dismay of many strikers, who didn't consider Murdoch's offer to be an acceptable form of settlement, Brenda Dean, Tony Dubbins and Norman Willis did not dismiss the offer out of hand.

The march was headed by the national leaders under a banner proclaiming: '6000 Sacked – News International Dispute'. But, soon after setting off, a clerical striker strayed too close to the banner and was firmly told by a steward to move away. His protestations, that he was one of the sacked 6000, receiving short shrift.

The head of the march finally reached the News International plant at Wapping and, for the first time in the dispute, the column filled the length and breadth of The Highway as far as the eye could see: a solid mass of people, placards and banners. The demonstration, which had been fairly subdued up to that point, suddenly burst into life, with the high walls on either side of the road at St Katherine's Dock acting as an echo chamber as the songs rang out. The police were out in strength, with every turning along The Highway, from Thomas More Street to Glamis Road, heavily guarded while, at the main entrance, they stood 10 deep with mounted back-up.

In Wellclose Square, opposite the entrance, an impromptu stage had been set up and from here miners' leader Arthur Scargill gave an impassioned speech, comparing the policing at Wapping with that of the miners' dispute and condemning the Conservative Government's attacks on trade unionists. He also questioned why he hadn't been invited to speak at Trafalgar Square!

By around 8.30pm, the crowds began to dwindle and late in the evening, when the lorries were leaving the plant, there were just a few hundred pickets left to deliver the customary verbal barrage. There was disappointment among the strikers that such large numbers of people had failed to affect the distribution of the papers, but the turnout had raised morale. They had also seen the lengths, through the massive police presence, to which the Government would go to protect Murdoch's position, but there was now a determined resolve that the two major demonstrations, planned for the start of May, should attract an even larger crowd.

The first mass meeting of sacked SOGAT members since the strike commenced took place at the Brixton Academy on 10th April. It had been called by the national union and strikers had been told that it would be for information purposes only. Around 800 people attended and despite the success, in terms of numbers, of the National Rally just four days before, Brenda Dean gave a very low key speech in which she intimated that the union was considering purging its contempt in the courts.

The poor turnout did not prevent those present from being highly critical of the way the dispute was being handled by the national union.

On the 12th April, Bruce Matthews, Managing Director of News International, announced that, in addition to the Gray's Inn Road offer, the company was willing to pay compensation to the sacked workers and, on the 16th, they met a delegation from the unions to inform them that they were prepared to pay £15million. The meeting was held at the Hyde Park Hotel in London, with a union delegation led by Brenda Dean and including Tony Dubbins. Murdoch was not present.

In a desperate effort to gain some form of recognition at Wapping, the unions proposed setting up a National Joint Council which would have trade union recognition, rather than individual unions. This would mean the end of the branch and chapel structures that had been built over the years. A single status deal was also offered, which meant there would be flexibility across the workforce.

The company's negotiators did not respond to the proposals for recognition at Wapping but, instead, stated that they were willing to extend the offer of part of the Gray's Inn Road building to the unions in the wider Labour Movement. This was a typical Murdoch tactic, as it would interest others who were not involved in the dispute, but could have undue influence on its outcome. The meeting ended with the company extending its offer until 30th May.

For the clerical strikers, meanwhile, two events occurred at the end of April which boosted their morale. Firstly, on the 24th, a court ruled that 60% of clerical branch funds should be released back to the branch and that only the 40% which was paid to the national union should remain sequestrated. This was good news because the staff employed by the branch were due to be made redundant soon as there would be no monies left to pay them. It also meant that the strikers, who were being asked to cover for the staff, could continue to concentrate on the strike.

On the following morning at around 8.30, approximately 300 strikers, most of whom were clericals, gathered at Wellclose Square, enjoying the spring sunshine and venting their anger on the shadowy forms of former colleagues hiding behind the window grills and blinds of the coaches turning into Virginia Street. Noting that there was only a modest police presence that morning, word spread concerning the unlikely possibility of approaching the plant's main gate. A few demonstrators dodged the fast-moving traffic and crossed The Highway, walked casually by the seemingly unconcerned policemen and, somewhat disbelieving, carried on towards the entrance.

Gradually, more people crossed the road, the trickle became a stream and finally, the traffic was brought to a standstill. Now the

Virginia Street pavement was thronging with people who spilled into the road at the bottom of the hill, blocking the huge iron gates at the entrance and taking the police and News International security staff completely by surprise. The large gates were closed, preventing access to the plant itself, but the mood was jubilant as the strikers stood, linked arms and began to sing. Scabs approaching the plant on foot were forced to walk down the middle of the road, escorted by police.

A coach carrying scabs had turned into Virginia Street and, as it was making its way towards the gate, the crowd surged towards it, banging on the sides and shouting at the occupants. The coach driver, realizing his predicament, turned his vehicle down Pennington Street and away from the plant. For the first time since the dispute began, scab workers had been stopped from entering the plant.

Then police reinforcements arrived, piling out of their white transit vans and pushing the crowd away from the gate onto the overcrowded pavement, which was hemmed in by railings on either side. The inevitable arrests followed as demonstrators would not, or could not, move as quickly as the police demanded. There was no violence on the strikers' side, the most animated incidents being the abuse of the scabs and a person clinging onto one of the protective grills of the coach.

As more police arrived, it was decided to make an orderly and honourable retreat, but the strikers were euphoric and, as word quickly spread beyond the picket line, the 'Taking of the Gate' became firmly established in strike folklore.

Although the clerical strikers had little interest in Murdoch's offer of a Labour Movement paper, they did become actively involved in running the strikers' own newspaper. *The Wapping Post* was set up by the London print union branches and several of the sacked News International journalists.

Carmel: *Initially, I went around scrounging typewriters and any other equipment to help get an office up and running. Keith Sutton, who had worked for the* Sunday Times Magazine, *and was Editor of the paper, encouraged me to write and after a while I started actually producing articles for the paper.*

The Wapping Post was popular amongst the strikers who felt starved of information about the dispute from the mainstream media, and it was distributed through a network of supporters around the country.

15

The May Rallies

The South East Region of the TUC organized the 1986 May Day Rally, with the News International dispute as its focal point. The chosen route was the obvious one: Tower Hill to the Wapping plant and there had been a big publicity effort. This included the distribution of a poster, designed by Tony Hall, one of the sacked workers, showing Murdoch quivering in a tree, with the masses approaching. The occasion and the publicity – and a rare day of glorious weather – ensured a good turn-out for a Thursday evening and, by 7pm, around 10,000 people had gathered at Tower Hill. Bands played and a large contingent from the Turkish community, waving red flags, led the singing as the march set off. There was a massive police presence at the main entrance to the Wapping plant and mounted police were situated at all the exit routes.

John: *The march had given everyone a real lift and the mood was very buoyant. But as we got nearer to the plant and saw the police on horse-back, wearing helmets and visors, the atmosphere changed. I was walking past Victoria Street, making my way along The Highway to Glamis Road, when something whizzed over my head and smashed through the window of a car. It's angle, its speed and the way it smashed the window suggested to me that it came from high up in the 'penthouse suites' that were being built along there. The building was behind police lines, facing the pickets.*

At around nine, attempts were made to move the marchers off The Highway at the plant entrance and back into Wellclose Square. The number of demonstrators was still fairly substantial at this time and the ordinary police had little success in clearing the road. Then, very suddenly, the mounted police were sent in to intimidate and disperse the demonstrators. There was resistance to the charges and missiles were thrown. They withdrew and a few minutes later riot police, armed with batons and shields, rushed into the crowd. The mounted police came in again behind them in attempts to drive people back and split them into smaller groups. Scuffles broke out and, once again, missiles were thrown. Police 'snatch squads' grabbed people in the ensuing mêlée and hit out at everyone who got in their way. Eventually, after several charges, they cleared

101

the road. While the police charges were taking place, the TNT lorries left the plant unhindered at Glamis Road.

Although the road at the plant entrance had been cleared, the police activity was by no means over. About an hour later, those demonstrators who remained were standing in Wellclose Square, or queuing at the tea vans. Without warning, the riot police, followed by mounted police with their batons drawn, surged into the Square. The stall run by Strike Graphics, which sold strike memorabilia, was smashed up with truncheons and people who had been quietly queuing for tea found themselves being chased and beaten by police. There was a lot of screaming and shouting, much of it from the riot police, who appeared to be in a state of frenzy.

This was the first time the 'safe' areas around Wellclose Square had been violated by the police – and for no apparent reason, other than to frighten and intimidate the demonstrators. It was an attempt to scare people off, to inhibit them from attending the much larger demonstration planned for May 3rd, when the 'Print Workers March for Jobs' was due to reach Wapping.

Madonna: *I'd been with my husband at Glamis Road for most of the evening, but by about 8.30 most of the demonstrators had made their way back to the main gate and we decided to join them. We were walking along The Highway when van loads of riot police went zooming past us. As we got within sight of the gate, we saw mounted police charging into demonstrators and riot police snatching people from the crowd. People were actually trying to fight back despite the fact that the police were carrying batons and shields and wearing hard hats. We were on the outside edge of the crowd now. There were loud shouts and screams and missiles began to be thrown in retaliation. The charges lasted several minutes and, eventually, they managed to force the crowd off the road. There was a great deal of anger and shock at the police behaviour and demonstrators continued to be arrested as they remonstrated with them.*

Over the next hour or so, people began to drift away, but a fairly large contingent remained in Wellclose Square, talking about the night's events. Suddenly, with no warning and for no reason, the riot police charged right into the Square, followed by mounted police with batons drawn. I was queuing for a cup of tea and as they lashed out my husband grabbed hold of me and we ran. We found ourselves being pursued by mounted police and I was so frightened I leapt into a building skip. I didn't climb in, I jumped. John followed and the police turned their attentions elsewhere. We were helpless as we watched people screaming and running all over the place. John wanted to go back and help, but I was terrified of being left alone, not knowing if he was ok.

After the police retreated there was a kind of stunned silence, but this was quickly replaced by anger. People were saying that it was just a warm up for Saturday (3rd May).

Next morning I was on a packed underground train on my way to work when a bloke next to me pulled out a copy of The Sun. *I just snapped. I ripped it out of his hands and screamed at him, 'do you know what happened last night so you could buy that crap today?' He was flabbergasted to say the least. I got off at the next stop and had a good cry. When I got to work I tried to explain, but I felt that nobody really believed me when I told them what had happened.*

One month earlier, the people who were to lead the 3rd May demonstration had set off on their long trek towards Wapping. At 10pm on Friday 4th April, 30 strikers drawn from each of the London branches of SOGAT and from the NGA, AUEW and NUJ, assembled at Euston Station to catch the night sleeper to Glasgow. The following week, a second group of strikers travelled to Ashington in Northumberland. They were embarking on the 'Print Workers March for Jobs'. The organization of the march was based on the TUC's 1983 'People's March For Jobs' and relied heavily on Regional TUCs looking after the marchers as they moved through each area, arranging overnight accommodation and meals, leafleting in advance of the marchers' arrival and agreeing routes and meeting sites with the local police. Stewards responsible for the discipline and conduct of the march were elected, along with those who would speak at rallies and give interviews and statements to the media. On the following evening at Murdoch's Kinning Park plant, accompanied by the stirring sound of pipes and drums, the first group set off on their journey to London.

Mick: *The night before the March, I went on a flying picket. It was pretty rough and when I came back I went into the picket office. They said to me, 'you'd better lie low for a while, why don't you go for a walk? Why don't you walk back from Glasgow?' I said, 'that sounds like a good idea'.*

We started from Euston. The train was delayed for a couple of hours because of a rail accident and we were in small groups because we didn't know the people from the other branches. The machine blokes had a laugh with us and nicked one of our bags – they took over straightaway. They had the majority of people on the march, but one person was elected from each branch and we all ended up having our say.

The people in Scotland received the shortest notice of any of the regions, but made first class arrangements for events, meals, accommodation and publicity.

Unfortunately, they took the marchers into the next region a day early, causing considerable problems for the Northern Region TUC – not to mention the marchers themselves.

There were some long stretches, especially near the beginning, and some of the schedules were ridiculous. During the first stage, someone was vomiting and had to go home. There was a big thing about crossing the border. We thought we were quite important at that stage and that the press would be there, so we learned some songs from a Rabbie Burns book to say goodbye to Scotland and hello to England. We sang them to each other to get them right and when we arrived, there were all these Scottish dignitaries. But no one from England turned up to greet us. Not one person from SOGAT!

An extra rest day had to be arranged in Carlisle to bring the marchers back on schedule and we stayed in a hall that was being renovated. There was no heating and we slept on a stone cold floor outside a ladies' toilet. The Tory council tried to evict us: they said we were being exploited. In the local paper the next day it said: 'Tory Councillor Says This is a Sham'.

On 22ⁿᵈ April, at Cannock, the Glasgow marchers joined up with the second group of marchers who had set out from Ashington and, on the 25ᵗʰ, we arrived at Northampton. This was the day that the clerical chapels 'took the gate' at Wapping.

Diedre: *On the day the clerical chapels 'took the gate', I went up to Northampton to meet the marchers. I had to tell them over and over and they were all getting geared up to do it themselves. I remember trying to explain to them that the police weren't expecting us to do it – that we weren't expecting us to do it! I tried to caution them.*

Tim: *It was something that built up, it was our goal: May 3ʳᵈ at Wapping. You didn't want to walk all the way down from Glasgow for nothing, go down to Wapping and shout 'scab'. That would have been daft. We knew it was going to be a big night and if there was going to be a delegation to the gate, it was going to be us.*

Mick: *At our last briefing we were told that we would lead the march down The Highway to the plant, where the other march, which would come down The Highway from the East, would meet us, then go up to the platform in Wellclose Square. After that we would walk down to the front and see what happened. We said no to a delegation to the gate in the end because we thought if anyone goes down there they'll be on a hiding to nothing.*

Graham: *As we got off the tube at Embankment, two machine men, aware that my wife would be going on the march with me, offered a word of warning. 'You be careful tonight, this is the big one!' There had been talk for a couple of weeks about '... going up the ramp', which implied that the head of the march* was intent on walking straight through the gate and up the elevated roadway used by the distribution lorries, into the plant. The chances of that happening seemed somewhat unrealistic and we thought little more about it. We saw the demonstration as a peaceful and legitimate means of protest.

The atmosphere outside Embankment station was carnival-like as work-mates and their families greeted each other and chatted excitedly as the procession slowly formed up in Arundel Street around the trade union banners. The Glasgow and Ashington marchers, wearing black baseball caps and luminous yellow jackets, were introduced by loud hailer and made their way triumphantly, with much back-slapping good humour and congratulations, to the front.

Helen: *I had been on the Ashington leg of the march. We didn't expect the welcome we got. When we marched up to the Embankment it was unbelievable. I can't explain how I felt. My family were there cheering with the rest of the crowd; people shouting hello and shaking our hands and kissing us. It makes me feel excited just thinking about it. We were treated like heroes – and we hadn't done anything except march.*

Maxine and I held the banner and led the march to Wapping. I have to admit, I felt so proud. Mind you that banner was heavy. Maxine kept saying 'how much further?' and I kept saying 'miles Maxine, miles'. We sang our marching songs all the way to Wapping. It was brilliant.

Tim: *When we got to the plant we were supposed to meet the other march coming from the East, but some official told us to go straight up to the square. Some of us didn't want to go; we wanted to meet the others in The Highway because we felt if we went up to Wellclose the whole thing would fizzle out. But it didn't work out that way at all. The other march didn't come and we were ferried up to Wellclose. We were all assembling there when the smoke bomb went off. There were police charges and everyone was screaming out, 'marchers stay there, keep together, we're going to calm it down'. But we couldn't stand there and watch it, I felt these people were there to support the 'March for Jobs' and we'd gone to the safe haven of the platform. 'I'm a marcher, I'm up here ok'. I couldn't stand there and see them getting a mashing. I just thought it was wrong. I got down the front. There were one or two throwing fencing but no serious injuries. At one time I was protecting a couple of girls against a police horse which was backing up and we were getting a real mauling. The girls were screaming and crying and I thought, 'I must be loony'.*

Mick: *What shocked us most was that we were standing on the platform when it happened. I didn't stay there too long, I couldn't just watch it because somehow I felt responsible for it – I felt guilty. I went down there ready to have a go at the police, I was really psyched up for it, but I was just shocked, I stood there like a dummy, I couldn't believe it. It did me in.*

Tim: *The adrenalin was there but it was the intensity of the fight against you. I'm in the front trying to do what I think is right, we're there to protest. But it was the intensity of people attacking you as if you are the enemy. You could probably get fifty accounts of what people wanted to do that night and they'd all be different. Those people who had whispered, the big machine blokes, their idea was that we would march down and some people would try for the gate. But when everybody went to the Square, everything changed anyway. I felt the intensity of the people attacking us was far greater than those who had some intent on our side.*

Graham: *As our section of the march slowly reached that part of The Highway that slopes down to the plant, we could see orange smoke near the police lines that were drawn up across the top of Virginia Street, which leads to the entrance. Suddenly, there was a lot of movement and disturbance ahead of us and we decided, as we had wives and children in our group, to make our way to the 'safe' area at the top of Wellclose Street. Pushing through the mass of people, we lost some of our companions and when we reached the union buses and tea vans, the children were ushered to safety by their grandparents. We stood at the top of Wellclose Square looking down past the speakers' platform towards the plant. All hell was breaking loose at the junction of The Highway and Virginia Street as the police horses charged repeatedly into the crowd. In the street behind us, some lads in woolly hats and 'combat' jackets were breaking up paving stones to use as ammunition against the police. Two elderly printers and their wives pleaded with them to stop, but the boys turned deaf ears – they were very excited and intent on 'getting the pigs'.*

Then there was a surge of movement up Wellclose Street and people were running past us shouting, 'they're coming, they're coming!' There was fear in the air, but we couldn't see what they were running away from and the rush subsided. A little later there was another, stronger surge. People scattered in all directions and leaped up onto the railing fence, pressing themselves flat against it in a pathetic attempt to hide themselves. Then we saw them: a wedge formation of maybe fifty policemen in full riot gear – black helmets with visors down; black overalls; truncheons drawn and round shields – surging round the corner into the Square. It was terrifying.

In retrospect, it reminded me of the television pictures I've seen of the running of the bulls in Pamplona. They are released to charge through the narrow streets of the town to the bull-ring and all the young men run ahead of them, the bravest just ahead of the charge. At Wapping the running was involuntary, the fear and panic just as real and, like Pamplona, there was nowhere to hide.

I pushed my wife back against the side of one of the caravans and stood over her, protecting her as best I could with my body. We stood still, expecting the worst. There was nothing else we could do. The sharp end of the police wedge stopped right beside us – not two feet away. They were screaming hysterically, 'down there, down there!' and after what seemed an eternity, charged past us into the square, laying about them on every side.

With my wife shaking uncontrollably, we made our way out of the back of the Square, only to be trapped by a mounted unit galloping down Cable Street. We slipped behind a fence into the flats and waited until they moved into the narrow street leading to the Square, deliberated and, to our great relief, turned back and rode off. We finally escaped and reached the car in Backchurch Lane.

Driving home, we passed the line of white TNT distribution vans – known as 'white mice' – waiting in the Mile End Road and listened to the first radio reports of the night's events. The earliest ones were accurate in emphasising the police violence, but by the time we sat drinking tea in my parents' living room, trying to explain to them – and ourselves – what had happened, the truth had receded under the welter of police casualty statistics.

After May 3ʳᵈ, my wife could never sleep until I got home from the demonstrations on Sunday Morning and it was New Year's Eve before she could bring herself to go to Wapping again.

Diedre: *I had arranged to meet C and my brother at the union bus at 10 o'clock. I was a bit late because of the trains and as I hurried down towards The Highway there were lots of people going home. I remember thinking, 'God, this is strange', because it was early even for the early crowd to be leaving. As I got closer to the plant I realised that all these people were crying. Children were crying and everyone looked white and ashen.*

I met a girl from The Sun *chapel and she asked me what she should do. I was just about to ask her what had happened when … It was like being in the middle of the Grand National, all these horses came charging up the road and we just ran. I didn't expect it to be totally peaceful, but – being three months pregnant – if I had known it was going to be that bad, I wouldn't have gone. But I had to stay because I had arranged to meet C and my brother. I thought, 'if I don't meet them they're going to be really worried about me'. I walked down that little alley by the green thinking that it was too narrow for the horses and I bumped into a friend of my dad's and he tried to drag me back to Tower Hill. I explained that I had to meet C and K, so he told me to stay where I was and he went off and found them for me. We walked up Dock Street to get to Cable Street. I stood there with C, we had our arms around each other's heads, face to face, as all the police horses charged by. We stood behind a car that had been turned over with the windows all smashed.*

We tried to get away from it, not away from Wapping – we were supposed to meet a coach load of Doncaster miners' wives who had come down to give us £250 they collected – but nowhere was safe from the rampaging policemen and horses and it was just impossible. It was like being on a 'Star Wars' set, all those anonymous people with black visors – and no identification. I remember the big lights scanning the flats, trying to identify people and eventually I got put on the union bus. I was upstairs because it was full of injured people downstairs. I sat up there with Brenda Dean. She was being interviewed.

Michele: *We were together – M and M, N and me – and as we were getting towards the plant I said to M, 'I've got a really strange feeling'. We both felt that something was going to happen, a really evil thing and yet, everybody was quite jolly and cheerful. Then, just as we got level with the entrance, MB (a SOGAT full time official) came up through the crowd and he was saying, 'go for the gate!' and he's pushing us all forward towards the gate, while he was going in the opposite direction towards Wellclose Square!*

We decided to get out of there as quickly as we could, so we got up to the Square, but were separated from M and M. Then the flares went up and the smoke and the horses came out. People were being crushed against the barriers but we were lucky and ran up around the back of the Square to the flats. From there we looked down on everything. It was packed with people, there were spotlights going on all over the place and the riot police came out. They were banging their shields, making this awful deafening, horrific noise like gorillas – and there was screaming. We couldn't go back into it – that would have been madness – and we couldn't go away from it. We just had to stand there and watch.

Helen: *All my family were there on May 3ʳᵈ to welcome me home, including my sister, a nurse, who was four months pregnant. One of the marchers collapsed by the stage. She was standing nearby and brought him round. But at that time I wanted her to leave him and get herself out because I was frightened for her safety. I got a few kicks and punches a couple of times but Maxine got beaten up. Some copper got hold of her head, put it under his arm and started beating her face. It was awful. She's only little.*

Denise: *As I was walking down on the march, there were so many of us I thought, 'tonight there's going to be trouble', because whenever there was a large number of people, the police seemed to attack to disperse you. There was an electric atmosphere. When the smoke bomb went off and the horses charged into The Highway, I climbed over the railings into the gardens at Wellclose Square. It's surprising what you can do in a panic. I stood in a corner by some bushes with a girl, two teenage boys and a middle-aged woman. The riot police came running through at first and the girl was getting upset. We were trapped in the Square for about 20 minutes, it might have been longer. I wasn't hit, I stood there as they ran into the enclosure, wielding their truncheons and I thought, 'they're just going to hit me indiscriminately. I'm going to get it in a minute', because they were just hitting people. I just stood there, there was nowhere else I could go. I thought, 'if I can climb back over the fence I can make my own way up to Thomas More Street and go home to my mum's, so I said to the girl, 'if we wait until it clears a bit I'll take you with me'. But then they came through the gate on horseback and she disappeared. I went out through the gate and ran all the way to my mum's flats a few streets away. I felt so angry. I didn't feel upset, I just felt angry.*

My mum wasn't in, so I knocked at my uncle's door and he had the telly on. He's a retired printer and he sits in his chair with his remote control. We watched it on the news and he said to me, 'I don't think you should go back there'. I said I'd go home, but I walked down Wapping Lane past the horses. I wanted to go back. I must have been gone about an hour and it looked like there had been a war, there was litter and bricks everywhere.

Joyce: *Come May 3rd, when the police charged up Wellclose Square and Brenda was still standing at the bloody microphone, I was shouting, 'sell out, sell out', and a woman in front of me asked me who I was. I said, 'I've been paying her wages for fifteen years, my name is Joyce, clerical. Who are you?' She said, 'I'm Brenda's secretary'. I said, 'why don't you answer my letter. You might have the courtesy to reply.'*

Pam: *I'd been away and came back that weekend. One of my neighbours was a printer and his daughter got married on the Sunday. It was a lovely wedding despite the strike and all his mates, also printers, had vowed not to say a word about the dispute during the proceedings. But because of what had gone on the night before, they couldn't help themselves and I heard all about it. It sounds silly, but I was sorry I hadn't been there. I felt almost guilty and was determined to go back to Wapping. It was meant to scare people off, but it made you feel even more determined.*

Frank: *3rd May really opened my eyes to what police action was all about. People had been dragged into the back of transit vans and beaten up. I wondered what was happening in our society. I'd been one of the majority, I suppose, who had not thought ill of the police previously and it came as a great shock. It was terrifying. I went to the flats behind Wellclose Square, thinking I was going to be safe there. But it was horrific even after the main assault was over. In the darkness, you could make out groups of riot police with their shields and helmets. There were groups of them everywhere and you thought, 'hell, there's no escape'. Where could you run to?*

SOGAT • NGA • AUEW • NUJ • SERTUC

PRINTWORKERS
MARCH FOR JOBS
GLASGOW/NEWCASTLE TO WAPPING

JOIN US ON

SATURDAY 3RD MAY
IN LONDON AT 7-30
ON THE EMBANKMENT

**FOR A MARCH TO WAPPING & A MASSIVE
NATIONAL RALLY OPPOSITE
'FORTRESS WAPPING'
AT 9. 00. pm.**

WE CALL UPON YOU FOR YOUR FULL SUPPORT ON
SAT. 3rd. MAY. WHEN WE MARCH INTO WAPPING.
BRING YOUR BANNERS AND YOUR FAMILIES, LET US
SHOW THE MURDOCHS AND THATCHERS OF THIS
WORLD THAT BRITISH PEOPLE ARE NOT UP FOR
SALE ON THEIR MONOPOLY BOARD

UNITED WE CAN WIN

16

The Offer Is Rejected

On 6th May, just three days after Brenda Dean described the Wapping confrontation as a 'Police Riot', the SOGAT National Executive purged its contempt of court, lifting the instruction to its members in the wholesale distribution sector not to handle the distribution of the News International publications. SOGAT members in London had continued to obey this instruction, but many wholesale members in the provinces, except initially in Glasgow and Merseyside, had ignored the union's instuction. In London, a fleet of white vans delivered directly to the newsagents, thus bypassing the 1,500 SOGAT wholesale workers and putting their jobs at risk. The 'white mice' as they became known, were targets for the strikers and, across London, bundles of *The Sun* and *News of the World* regularly disappeared after being delivered to newsagents' doors.

The conditions attached to purging the contempt included an agreement not to intimidate News International employees, or interfere with the running of their business. On the back of the decision, a rift that had been developing between the national union, the London branches and their striking members had become a large chasm. The London District Council (LDC) issued a press release condemning the National Executive's decision, adding that they intended to escalate the dispute, and a mass meeting of the SOGAT strikers was announced, with the intention to call for support for the proposed escalation

On the 19th May around 300, mainly clerical, strikers marched down Fleet Street and Gray's Inn Road, passing the offices of several national newspapers and their own former places of work. They were making their way to the mass meeting of strikers at Westminster and were determined to remind other Fleet Street workers that the dispute was still very much alive. The second mass meeting since the confident, defiant affair at Brixton, just prior to the start of the dispute, took place in the opulent splendour of Central Hall, Westminster. The meeting was called by the LDC to present their proposals for an escalation of the dispute by increasing both the number of demonstrations at Wapping and the national picketing operations. The previous week, Brenda Dean had written to the LDC scolding them for their plans. She reminded them of the guarantees that had been given to the judge when the National Executive had taken the decision to purge their contempt and release the union from sequestration.

Two thousand angry printers were making a tumultuous din when George Holmes, chairman of the LDC, called for any non-union members to leave the hall. Immediately, the cry of 'stranger' went up and a quivering individual in the gallery made a hasty exit. There were also strong objections to the announcement that no other proposals, apart from the LDC's four point plan, would be heard at the meeting. The chairman was unable to bring the meeting to order for several minutes and when Brenda Dean finally got to her feet, she was greeted with howls of derision. In her autobiography she states that, although she was listed on the publicity for the meeting, she was never officially invited. She also claimed that the police had contacted her to express concerns for her safety and that there were plain clothes police present at the meeting.

Her address was very low key and met with much hostility from the strikers. She reported on the meeting that had taken place with News International on 16th April, following Murdoch's offer of part of the Gray's Inn Road building to print a Labour Movement newspaper. She also gave details about the concessions that had been offered by the unions to gain recognition at Wapping. These concessions and the acceptance of the conditions attached to the purging of the union's contempt, were seen by many of those present as a betrayal.

Boos and heckling from the strikers continued throughout her report, but she ended by saying she would take questions from the floor, take notes, and reply after all the questions had been asked.

George Hall, the Clerical FOC from NGN, was the first to speak and it was noticeable, even from the gallery, that his notes were shaking in his hand. In his condemnation of the union leadership's conduct and commitment to the strike, he set the tone for all the other speakers. The climax was reached when a distraught Machine Branch member, seemingly close to tears, accused Brenda Dean and the SOGAT sponsored Labour Party MP Ron Leighton of refusing to heed repeated pleas during the demonstration, on 3rd May, for them to ask the police to allow a heart attack victim out of Wapping. Referring to them repeatedly as 'film stars', he insisted they had excused themselves by saying that they were due to deliver speeches from the platform.

At the end of all this, obviously shaken by the depth of hostility, Brenda Dean answered only those questions she chose, denying any knowledge of the heart attack victim. Then the whole union executive, offering the excuse of a prior engagement, stood up and filed off the platform, accompanied by cries of 'resign'.

After this turmoil, the LDC document was accepted by the meeting, but without the proper airing that it warranted. However, the LDC's position made little difference to the negotiations going on behind the scenes.

On Monday 26th May it was suddenly announced that secret talks had been going on over that weekend between the company and the unions, which included the EETPU. The company offered both Gray's Inn Road buildings and compensation for each sacked worker (four weeks salary at a maximum of £155 per week for every year of service). This equated to £50 million in compensation. Not surprisingly, there was to be no union recognition at Wapping, although the proposals stated that this would be reviewed in 12 months. In addition, a token gesture was made allowing sacked workers to apply for any vacancies that occurred at the plant.

The strikers were furious when Brenda Dean and Norman Willis, rather than a company spokesperson, announced that this was Murdoch's final offer. To add insult to injury, the SOGAT National Executive were not going to recommend acceptance or rejection of the offer. For his part Murdoch, in what appeared to be a co-ordinated effort with the unions, said they had pushed him hard to get what he had given. That he didn't have to give anything, but wanted to assist the strikers.

The clerical chapels reacted quickly to the news of the offer and organized a chapel meeting for the 29th May. The venue was the Oliver Thomson Lecture Theatre at City University, and in order to encourage a good attendance, the meeting was held at 6.30pm. A packed auditorium listened to many calls for a 'No' vote and, at the end of a very positive meeting, a motion was passed recommending the rejection of Murdoch's offer and urging the chapel to take all appropriate steps to escalate the dispute with News International.

Joyce: *It was the first offer and I'd read all the stuff about what the union offered Murdoch, which was most of what he'd asked for, and I was in tears.*

We'd been down there for four months getting our heads bashed in and Brenda Dean had done this. I was raging. I sat at the typewriter and wrote a letter to her. My opening sentence was: 'Brenda, my first inclination is to rip up my SOGAT card and send it to you with a none too polite instruction as to what to do with the remnants. What do I tell my children? My son is on the picket line with me. What do I tell the people in the Print Workers Support Group and all the people who have nothing to do with the dispute, but come down to Wapping to support us? What do I tell them after what you've done?'

The ballot forms were to be sent directly by the national union to the strikers' home addresses, a decision which was challenged in the courts by the London Machine Branch (LMB). The union rules stated that ballots should be distributed via the individual branches, but a High Court judge rejected the LMB's case, the ballot process continued and the divisions with the national union intensified. The ballot form was accompanied by a letter from Brenda Dean giving details of the offer, but making no recommendations on which way to vote. The letter did not include the supplementary points which, according to press reports, had been agreed with the company. These included that the print unions 'would not take further disciplinary action against those who did not take strike, or any other form, of industrial action, and would cancel any disciplinary action or proceedings to date'. Within a few days, another letter arrived from the General Secretary denying that any agreement had been reached with the company about the unions taking disciplinary action against the scabs.

Prior to the ballot result being announced on 6th June, two significant events occurred. On the 2nd, a morning demonstration at Wapping took place and around 300 strikers, a large number of whom were women, marched across The Highway and down to the main gate, where they remained for the next two hours. During this time, scab coaches and cars were prevented from entering the plant and reel lorries were prevented from exiting. Suddenly, Bruce Matthews and others were spotted on a rooftop inside the plant. The demonstrators produced a loud hailer and made it clear to him that they would not be walking away from the dispute. As police numbers increased, the strikers marched off down Pennington Street, then on to Wapping Lane and The Highway, where the traffic was brought to a halt until the police managed to clear the road.

Late on that same night, a blaze started at News International's

Convoys Wharf paper warehouse at Deptford, in South-east London, which supplied paper to Wapping and a number of other national and provincial newspapers. It destroyed part of a warehouse, 9,000 tons of paper and trucks worth £7 million. Firemen were still fighting the fire on the following day, but were unable to reach the centre of the warehouse to start investigating the cause. This didn't stop Bruce Matthews, standing amongst the smouldering embers, saying on breakfast-time television that he had no doubt that the fire had been started by printers. He also referred to 'the violent picketing' at Wapping the previous morning. Matthews suggested that violence was being used to achieve a 'No' vote in the ballot. The company offered a £50,000 reward for information leading to an arrest and conviction.

Scotland Yard said it was treating the incident as a probable case of arson, saying that two local women had reported seeing two men hurl something into the building. A spokesman for Convoy's said the layout of the building and the denseness of the newsprint reels made it unlikely that such a massive fire could start, or spread so quickly, from a simple incendiary device. 'It was a very professional job. I am only speculating, but it appears that something such as petrol was thrown over some of the reels', he said.

In a joint statement, SOGAT and the NGA said:

> 'The unions have no involvement with the fire. If it was started deliberately, we completely condemn such action. We also deplore the provocative statements made, without any evidence, by Rupert Murdoch's representative, that there was no doubt that the blaze was started by print workers with whom the firm is in dispute. This is finding our members guilty by association and the allegations should be substantiated or withdrawn.'

After a five-hour meeting, the FOCs /MOC's of the striking chapels issued a statement saying:

> 'These allegations attempt to portray trade unionists as thugs and criminals. This is unacceptable and unjust. SOGAT had instructed firemen, who are SOGAT members, to remain at News International's Bouverie Street and Gray's Inn Road buildings, to protect the safety conditions of those still employed there.'

Privately, reported *The Guardian*, London Branch officials of SOGAT felt that the fire would damage the chances of securing a vote to reject the company's final offer of £50 million compensation for the sacked workers.

Nobody was ever charged in connection with the fire.

The next few days at Caxton House were very tense. Rumours implied that people hadn't received their ballot forms and, with relationships at a low point, conspiracy theories as to why the national union would not allow any of the strikers to observe the count were rife.

At around 6pm on Friday 6th June, the ballot result was announced from SOGAT's headquarters at Hadleigh in Essex. The offer was rejected, with 2081 voting against and 1415 in favour. The clerical chapels had voted to reject the offer by 280 to 141. The NGA voted to reject the offer by a majority of four to one.

John: *There was a mood of real jubilation at Caxton House when the result came through: hoards of television crews and reporters from the dailies fussed around on the street outside, and lots of very happy strikers were willing to speak to them. When I got home later that night, I watched the television coverage. Brenda Dean seemed genuinely disappointed with the result.*

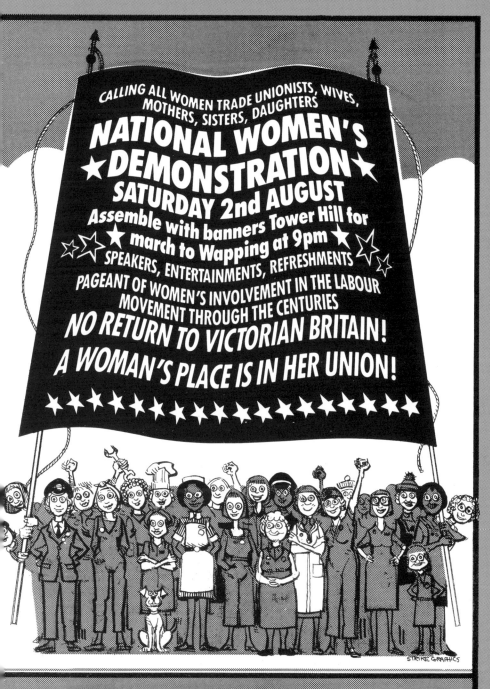

Organised by the SERTUC Womens' Rights Committee
in support of sacked News International workers

Printed by Trojan Press Ltd (T.U.) 01-249 5771

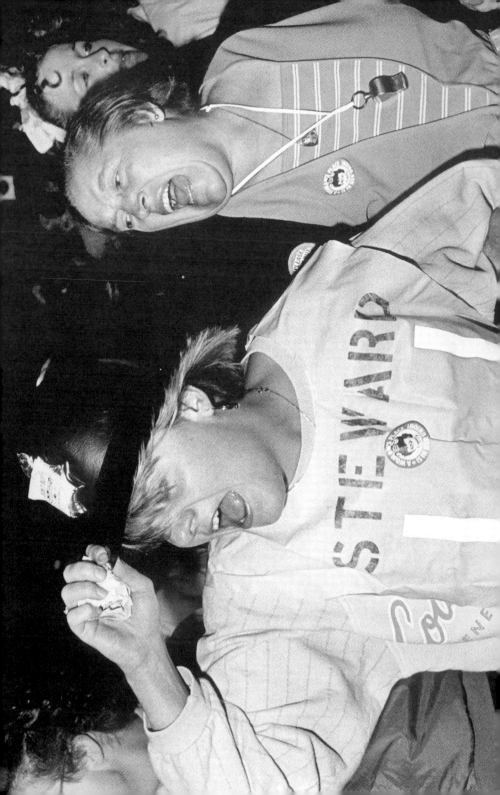

17

The Conference and the Courts

With the offer rejected, there was an expectation among the strikers that the dispute would be escalated. Unfortunately, these expectations did not last long: two days after the result was announced, the SOGAT Biennial Delegate Conference commenced in Scarborough. Around 50 clerical strikers arrived by coach to lobby delegates and they encountered a somewhat hostile reception. This was partly due to a remark made to the press by Brenda Dean on the previous day, when she said that it would be bad for the London branches to break away from the union. The possibility of a breakaway had never been discussed at meetings, or on the picket line. Her remark came out of the blue and was never clarified.

In addition, the cause was not helped by allegations that some strikers who arrived a few days earlier had, through a mixture of frustration and alcohol, been verbally aggressive towards delegates.

The key day for the strike was on the 12th June, when the Emergency motions regarding the dispute were debated: Brenda Dean moved Motion No.8 on behalf of National Executive Council, which asked the Biennial Delegate Council to:

- Accept the ballot result on the offer put forward by News International.
- Support the continuation of the dispute and pursue it with all possible means consistent with ensuring the maintenance of SOGAT as an independent trade union.
- Confirm that the dispute will come under direct responsibility of the National Executive Council in accordance with the rules of the Society.
- Confirm the stepping up of the boycott campaign, seeking the support of all trade unions to ensure its success.
- Direct that, for the duration of the dispute, all branches in the society be involved and be regularly consulted.
- Call upon the TUC to continue to press for an acceptable negotiated settlement with the company.

As well as calling for more support from the other SOGAT branches and other trade unions, she emphasised that the dispute

◀ *A clerical striker (wearing a plastic policeman's helmet) stewarding a women's march at Wapping (2/8/86). (David Hoffman Photo Library)*

would 'go forward with renewed vigour … under the banner of the National Executive Council'.

She spoke at length of the financial damage that had been caused to the union whilst it had been in sequestration and made it clear that the NEC did not 'intend to allow the courts, or sequestrators to take this union from us'.

With the conditions laid down by the court when purging the union's contempt (including agreement not to intimidate News International employees, or interfere with the running of their business) the national union's support for the continuation of the dispute was to focus on the stepping up of the boycott campaign.

She stated that 'the boycott campaign has got to have one single message behind it: that no decent human being in this country today should buy *The Sun, News of the World, The Times* or *Sunday Times* until our members get a just settlement'.

From the strikers' point of view, the boycott campaign had been an abject failure. Now it was being proposed as the essential tool in the fight with Murdoch.

Graham: *No matter how often I gave out strike leaflets in the street, I always felt somehow naked, a target to be shot at, expecting to be challenged to justify the dispute by every passer-by. In reality though, very few people actually did confront you and many, if the look on their faces were anything to go by, felt challenged themselves as you invaded, just for a moment, their cosy insularity. Most people simply snatched the leaflet and hurried on, while others looked at you as though you'd just crawled out of the gutter and wouldn't accept one at any price.*

It was like a slap in the face every time you saw somebody reading The Sun *– and you saw somebody reading* The Sun *every minute of the day. You knew that millions of people read it, but it didn't make it any easier. You just realized that people didn't give a shit about it.*

Frank: *The average person didn't really want to know. My neighbours used to ask me what was happening and I used to explain. They would listen sympathetically, didn't say much, and I don't think they were really very interested. But my family were very supportive.*

I think the boycott campaign was a loser. It's a great pity it didn't take off and have some effect. When you were on the street, 50% of people refused to accept the leaflets. Unfortunately, most of the public didn't want to know, partly because of the long years of propaganda about over-paid Fleet Street workers. For years there had been a belief among the general public that if you worked on a newspaper you were one of these three nights a week, £40,000 a year people. So we reaped the consequences. It was 'serves you bloody well right, you've had it too good for too long'.

Having made it clear that the union would not allow itself to be sequestrated again, Brenda Dean announced that the NEC was opposed to the next emergency motion on the conference agenda. This was to be proposed by the London Machine Branch and asked that 'this conference calls upon all of our members, whether involved in printing or distribution, to support our dismissed members by not printing or distributing News International titles'.

Carmel: I was part of the London District Council delegation, as I was supposed to be presenting a report to the conference regarding the role of women in the union. During Brenda Dean's speech, there was a lot of heckling from the London delegates, including myself, as we were very unhappy about her commitment to the dispute and we could see ourselves becoming more and more isolated. Things got even more hostile when she announced that the London Machine Branch motion would not be supported.

At this stage the branch secretary of the London Clerical Branch requested a 15 minute adjournment in order for the London delegates to meet to discuss their response to the NEC's motion. They were faced with the prospect of voting against their own union, with the vote still being carried by the rest of the conference delegates. In addition, their own motion (via the London Machine Branch), to escalate the dispute looked certain to be rejected. After 15 minutes of heated debate and arguments, they returned to say that they would be supporting the NEC motion, which was duly carried without opposition.

The London Machine Branch motion was still put forward with the mover of the motion, Tony Isaacs of *The News of the World*, informing the conference that he had every right to have a go at the members of the National Executive as 'I pay their bloody wages'. He also predicted that the union would be sequestrated again within a week or two even 'in regard to the boycott'. Brenda Dean opposed the motion on behalf of the NEC and forcibly pointed out that the 'union would be in contempt if we reapplied that instruction' (not to print or distribute News International titles). Then she turned her attention to the seconder of the motion, Roy 'Ginger' Wilson. Wilson was the Father of the Chapel of *The Sunday Times* machine branch chapel and was known to a number of the clerical chapel members (especially those who worked in the cashiers department where the wages were paid out on a Saturday night) as being loud and aggressive. He had been a vocal supporter of Brenda Dean at the meeting in Brixton in January, when she had called for strike action. But their relationship had soured since then.

Wilson had made a rambling speech, with comments about people who had been earning £300 to £350 per week who were now 'finished, with no money coming in and with bailiffs selling up their houses'. Talk of this kind of money would have further alienated delegates from the provinces, but Brenda Dean had even more damning information: like many printers on national newspapers, Wilson was employed by a daily (*The Daily Express*) as well as a weekend paper. She was currently involved in negotiations with the *Daily Express*, where she had found out that Wilson had recently taken voluntary redundancy. She announced this fact to the conference, pointing out that she found it 'damned difficult to convince the world out there that it is about jobs, when one of our leading lights took £26,500 of voluntary redundancy pay in the middle of the dispute, from his other employer!' For once, the normally vocal Wilson was silent. He received no support from his fellow London delegates and the motion was lost.

With their offer rejected, News International turned to the courts once more, to try to break the dispute. On 16th June, writs were issued against SOGAT and the NGA and also against several individuals. These included the clerical branch secretary, Chris Robbins, Bill Freeman and Michael Hicks. Freeman and Hicks were members of the London District Council, and the Communist Campaign Group (CCG). Although neither was on strike, they had both developed a high profile during the dispute. Freeman, a down to earth and sociable man, was a committee member at *The Observer*. During the week, however, he was based at Caxton House, where he was the main organizer in the National Picketing Office. Hicks was the Imperial FOC at John Menzies, one of the main wholesale distribution companies. His members were directly affected by the dispute as they were being bypassed by News International's scab distribution system. He regularly appeared at the demonstrations at Wapping, megaphone in hand, performing what could be described as a master of ceremonies role. He would give speeches, introduce other speakers and lead the singing until, invariably, the police moved in to clear the road outside of the plant. Both men were liked by the majority of the strikers as they were seen as offering genuine resistance to Murdoch.

Behind the scenes, however, striking clerical committee members had disagreements with both men and another member of the CCG, Ann Field, who was assistant branch secretary of the clerical branch. She had previously been an MOC at *The Times* and, like Hicks and Freeman, was a popular figure amongst many of the strikers. The committee felt that the CCG had their own political agenda and that they were having undue influence on the direction of the strike. This sometimes culminated in very vocal arguments at the weekly FOC's/MOC's meetings

Whilst waiting for the court cases to start, events continued on the ground. The day after the writs were issued, the main gate at Wapping was 'taken' once more, this time by around 300 demonstrators. Others blocked The Highway and, it being a Tuesday afternoon, it was not long before traffic jams began to build up. Mounted police charged the demonstrators at the main gate and several arrests were made.

The resulting court cases eventually commenced on the 9th July and, on the same day, the National Executive Committee ordered the National Picket Office to be closed down. This instruction was issued following damage, allegedly caused by flying pickets, to a TNT depot at Eastleigh in Hampshire, on the 6th July. The national union was determined to keep the union out of the hands of the sequestrators and show the courts that, by issuing such instructions, they could control the strike. In addition, the national union referred to the 'rogue' behaviour of individuals.

A mood of despondency and isolation prevailed among many of the clerical strikers around this time. They felt their national union had deserted them and that the promised development of the boycott campaign had not, unsurprisingly, materialized since it was heralded by Brenda Dean at the conference a month earlier. In addition to this, the national union announced that it was to cut their strike pay from £12 to £6 per week. This followed the decision, during the previous week, that the strike pay from the branch was also to be cut. In addition, the facilities at Caxton House began to be withdrawn and the branch secretary confirmed that the Operations Room would close at 8pm every evening except Saturdays. With more people being placed into work, it was not surprising that those remaining active within the dispute felt despondent.

In an effort to lift the mood and give the dispute fresh impetus, the clerical committee put forward proposals to be taken to a mass meeting of strikers planned for 19th July. At a meeting of the clerical strikers on the 18th, two motions were passed: the first called for the London District Council to implement the equalization of strike pay. This was a bug bear for the clericals as their branch had, since the on-set of the dispute, paid its striking members far less than the other branches. This highlighted the fact that the old demarcation lines that had existed in the workplace had continued during the strike.

The second motion was far more contentious as it proposed the election of a strike committee, which would comprise four striking members from each of the London branches, plus four NGA, two AEU and two NUJ strikers. The committee, which would meet weekly, was to be elected by, and be accountable to, the mass meetings of strikers and would replace the FOC's and MOC's meeting, which took place every Tuesday. These meetings were quite often attended by upwards of 50 people and had little or no structure. Some of those present were not strikers, but various officials from the London branches. There was a lot of speech making but, considering the hours that were spent, few constructive decisions were made about the running of the dispute.

The mass meeting took place on a Saturday afternoon at York Hall in Bethnal Green and was very poorly attended, with only around 300 strikers present. The clerical motions were the only ones on the agenda and the first, calling for the equalization of strike pay, was passed unopposed, but with plenty of abstentions. However, the second motion, calling for the formation of a strike committee caused a much greater stir. Numerous FOCs took affront at the proposal and how it undermined their authority. The motion was soundly defeated, but at least it allowed some genuine debate about how the dispute was being run.

John: *After the mass meeting, Ann Field told me that she was disgusted that our chapels had proposed such a motion and that she was going to come along to our next chapel meeting and sort it out! I told her it was called democracy.*

This was not the first time that the clerical strikers had disagreed over the direction of the dispute. From the outset, the TNL and NGN clerical committees had called for the strike to be escalated to the rest of Fleet Street. Newspaper proprietors had a poor record in supporting each other and it was felt that, with their own publications being affected, they would put pressure on Murdoch to settle the dispute on terms favourable to the strikers. It would also send out a clear message to the other proprietors that they should not consider attempting to implement the same terms and conditions that Murdoch had sought. Although the clerical strikers voted in favour of a 'Fleet Street Out' policy, there were differences of opinion as to whether, if implemented by the national union, it could be successful.

John: *Brenda Dean should have gone into Fleet Street and ordered them out. It was her place and that's what she should have done. But, in the end, we were trying to force her to do it. It would have been against the law, but we were going to be sequestrated again anyway, because of the restrictions placed on demonstrating, so it didn't really matter. There was a lot of apathy in The Street, but she had to stop the other papers printing. I honestly don't believe the other proprietors would have allowed Murdoch to be the only one with his papers on the streets. They would have forced him back around the table for a settlement. If it had been done early on, the settlement would have been more favourable to the workforce, even though Brenda would have accepted almost anything on our behalf, to get into that plant.*

Joyce: *It was said that we should get the whole of Fleet Street out, but I still have my doubts about that. Without 100% support in the right areas, it would have been a disaster. If Murdoch's opposition was off the streets he would have cleaned up. The other argument is that the proprietors had never been able to stick together and there was no way that the likes of Stevens, Maxwell and Black would have allowed him to do that. They didn't have an alternative work-force like Murdoch, so their papers would have been off the streets. It would have needed her to go into the Street and I don't think she ever did. She didn't know Fleet Street, she didn't understand it, she didn't have an affinity with it.*

People have suggested bad things about Brenda, but I don't think she's a bad person. I don't seriously think she would have let it happen solely to teach London a lesson. It might have happened as a by-product. It turned out to her advantage, but I don't think she would have done it at the human cost and the financial cost to the union's coffers. But, at the same time, she was out of her depth.

The striking clerical chapels failed to convince their national union or any of the other London branches (including their own) to adopt this policy.

Within two weeks of the strike commencing, both *The Guardian* and

Associated Newspapers, publishers of *The Daily Mail, Mail on Sunday* and *London Standard*, had announced that they intended to move production of their newspapers from Fleet Street over the course of the next two years. This would involve the introduction of computerized typesetting and the loss of several hundred jobs. The national unions and the London branches decided that they would not use this as an opportunity to link these announcements to the News International dispute and, instead, chose to negotiate agreements for the moves.

As the strike continued, other proprietors revealed their plans to move their publishing and editorial facilities out of Fleet Street. As each announcement was made, the News International strikers became more and more isolated. The deals that were eventually concluded with the other newspapers contained agreement on many of the issues that the News International workers had taken strike action over and eradicated many of the terms and conditions that had been fought for over the years.

The mood was not helped when Neil Kinnock, the Labour Party leader, chose to write an article for *The Sunday Times*. Perhaps it should not have come as a surprise, but many of the strikers remembered his scathing attack on Murdoch at the rally in support of the dispute held at the Wembley Conference Centre just four months earlier.

Despite the feeling that the dispute was in decline, occasionally events took place that gave everybody a lift. On 23rd July, the day Prince Andrew and Sarah Ferguson were married, an 'Alternative Royal Wedding', complete with stalls, side-shows, comedians and singers took place at Wapping. The event, which encouraged families to attend, was billed as 'The Ragged Trousered Cabaret' and the publicity stated that it would take place between 4pm and 9pm on the Green at Wellclose Square. However, an unpublicized demonstration took place at 2pm, catching the police, at full stretch due to the real ceremony at Westminster Abbey, completely off guard. Around 2,000 demonstrators set off from Tower Hill and within a few minutes traffic in the area was brought to a standstill. With enough people to cover all exits, a lorry carrying reels of paper to the plant was delayed trying to enter Wapping Lane from The Highway. Some demonstrators climbed onto to the back of the vehicle, cut the straps holding the huge reels of paper and succeeded in kicking two reels off into the road. Police eventually arrived to rescue the lorry, which drove into Wapping Lane with the remainder of its load balancing precariously.

It took around an hour for the police to muster their forces and The Highway was eventually cleared when mounted officers charged into the crowd. Most of the demonstrators regrouped at Tower Hill at around 5pm and were joined by many others making their way to the official event. They set off towards the plant and once again the march blocked The Highway.

To facilitate the surprise element, no banners were taken to the earlier demonstration, but the Lesbian and Gay Print Workers Support Group arrived for the official march proudly carrying theirs. The banner, however, was quickly taken up by two burly printers and some 200 strikers fell in behind and marched up to the police lines in Virginia Street, where they were met by homophobic jibes from the police ranks. The strikers retorted with: 'we know who the enemy is and it's not lesbians and gays'.

On the 31st July, the result of the court case was announced: restrictions on the way picketing and demonstrations could be carried out at Wapping, Bouverie Street, Gray's Inn Road and the TNT depots were imposed. But fears that the picketing of the main gate at Wapping would be stopped (the anti-union laws made it clear that you could not picket premises that were not your place of work) proved unfounded and the court stated that a maximum of six pickets at the gate would be allowed to continue.

Further restrictions demanded that The Highway should not be obstructed, that pickets should not indulge in any form of intimidation, including shouted insults and abuse, and that there should be no violence of any form directed at either persons or property. Pickets were also instructed not to try to persuade those working in the plant to cease. However, they were allowed to talk to people entering or leaving the plant (if those people were willing to talk to the pickets) solely for the purposes of communicating or receiving information concerning the dispute.

SOGAT and the NGA were ordered by the court to instruct their members within 72 hours of the terms of the orders. By the following day, Brenda Dean had written to all of the Branch Secretaries directing them to inform all chapel officials and members of the terms of the orders. In her letter, she stated that 'members are reminded of the motion passed at the Biennial Delegate Council which directed that no steps should be taken by the union which might jeopardize its independence and put it back into the hands of the sequestrators'. She continued: 'The Executive Council wishes to make it clear that it cannot countenance any action by any officer or member which constitutes a breach of any of the orders' and that the union would be 'required to take disciplinary action against any officer or member who takes action which infringes any of the orders and thereby places the position of the union in jeopardy'. She also pointed out that if individuals acted 'in a manner inconsistent with the orders, they may be personally in contempt of court and liable accordingly'.

Finally, she directed that 'as from the date of this letter all picketing, demonstrations and marches at or near the vicinity of the Murdoch premises at Wapping, Bouverie Street and Gray's Inn Road must not be organized, save by the Executive Council itself, or with its express consent. The dispute with News International continues, but it is pointed out that this must be concluded within the terms of the order attached'.

The letter re-affirmed the national union's determination not to be sequestrated but also, for the first time, threatened disciplinary action (and possible court action) against its striking members. No disciplinary action had been taken by the union against the scabs, and any doubts that the strikers were being left to 'wither on the vine' could now be well and truly dispelled.

The anger and bitterness that had built up against News International over the previous six months was now being directed at their own union. Those strikers who remained active in the dispute felt isolated and many believed the union would end the dispute at the first opportunity. They also believed that only their own actions would force News International to make an acceptable offer to settle the dispute.

On 1ˢᵗ August, the day after the court judgment, *The Evening Standard* reported that a TNT depot at Thetford in Norfolk had been 'attacked by a crowd of more than 200' who 'threw bricks and stones, causing more than £10,000 worth of damage'. The article continued 'a dozen workers' cars and 15 delivery vans were damaged during an hour of mayhem in which attackers lit fires outside the depot and aimed flares at an office block. The crowd fled as police arrived, but not before breaching the fence around the depot in two places. Inside the grounds, attackers damaged vans and set fire to bundles of papers. No arrests were made'.

Mick: *The first flier was about two weeks into the dispute. There were about 20 of us, all clericals, in the back of a hired vegetable van. We nearly froze to death. It was a TNT supplements depot and there was a Trades Council picket there from day one. We went to bolster the numbers and raise morale.*

Tim: *There were two car-loads for the second one – eight people – and I knew it was going to be serious. There was a winding road, about two miles long, on an industrial estate, and we had to drive down it to the place. We drove to a lay-by where the other lads were waiting and sneaked along a little gully at the back of the factory and through the wire. A few of us went through and did a bit of business, a few windows and a slashed a tyre which went off like a rocket, and a security bloke came out of his hut, walking nearer and nearer to us. The consensus was to do a runner, so we did. But he ran after us. We were running like hell when our two cars came along, lights off and doors open, like something out of The Sweeney.*

There was only ever talk about assaulting anyone. It was when we were actually planning to take over a depot. It was talked about, the numbers were worked out, but it was called off.

But the fliers were about damaging property, not people. We were not in dispute with the people. But, in the end, the pressure got to them and the lorry drivers were wearing crash helmets. On Saturday nights people would say, 'you're shooting off a bit early' and you'd say, 'yes, I'm a bit knackered'. They thought you'd shot off to the pub, but you'd be up till four in the morning on a flier. You couldn't tell anybody.

Pam: *I thought the fliers were great. I had no qualms about property being damaged, I felt quite vindictive. You got so frustrated because you weren't allowed to do anything effective. If you heard that someone had managed to pull something off, it was a bit of a triumph. It was just a rage, how else can you explain it. It was pure frustration. Whatever you tried to do, they beat you back. We weren't making any progress, just getting more and more frustrated. You felt the whole machinery was against you. It wasn't just Murdoch and us was it, all the papers were maligning us, and that leaves a bitter taste that will take a long time to get rid of.*

Frank: *Quite honestly, the fliers were all so secretive I didn't know much about them. Obviously, those people concerned wouldn't talk about it. You might be at the branch and people would start arriving and go down into the basement. It was all very clandestine and you never heard very much about what they got up to. But I think it was fair game, because the changes in the law made striking virtually illegal and if you did go on strike you could do so little. We were deprived of all our basic freedoms to demonstrate and to strike. I don't agree with the ban on secondary picketing: it's a basic right to withdraw your labour and if, in order to pursue that right, you have to demonstrate outside a building that is not your workplace, then you should have a right to do so. I don't know much about what the flying pickets did, maybe some of the things were a bit rough but, in principle, I think they had a right to do it. You have to take the fight to the enemy.*

On the 2nd August, around 6,000 people attended a 'Women's March'. The turnout gave the strikers a much needed boost and was seen as a positive response to the court decision. Taking advantage of this mood, a lunchtime demonstration outside the Gray's Inn Road building was arranged by the strikers on August 5th as a direct response to the national union's instruction that they alone would organize demonstrations.

A large crowd of over 500 ensured that the main road was blocked and that those trying to enter or leave the building were unable to do so. Feeling buoyed by this success, the demonstrators marched along Gray's Inn Road and down to Fleet Street, where their singing and chanting brought workers from other newspapers out onto the street. The demonstrators halted at the Bouverie Street building to let the scabs inside know they had not gone away, and the march then proceeded to Wapping, bringing traffic to a standstill along the way. The demonstration ensured that the court orders were breached and the strikers awaited the response from the company and their union.

They didn't have to wait long: the following day, a further list of instructions arrived from the national union, signed by the General President, Danny Sergeant. Whilst reiterating much of Brenda Dean's letter, certain parts went beyond the actual court order. Sergeant stated that 'only workers involved in the dispute should participate in the daily demonstrations and other groups and individuals not connected with the dispute should be asked to leave the demonstration immediately'. This implied that a member of one's own union (or branch) who was not directly involved in the dispute, should be told that they were not welcome.

A similar instruction was issued with regard to the marches and demonstrations at Wapping, with Sergeant stating that: 'only people with a direct interest in the dispute should attend on the demonstrations and marches. Other groups and individuals not connected with the dispute should be asked to leave the march or demonstration straightaway'.

Sergeant attended the regular FOC's/MOC's meeting on the 7th August at which he tried to justify the instructions.

John: *I asked a few questions, including what would happen to those people who disobeyed the instructions? After much dithering, he said that if the instructions were being broken deliberately, disciplinary action would be taken against them. There was a lot of anger at the meeting and, at one point, I accused the General President of being a liar. After a couple of hours, he tried to walk out, but his way was blocked and he had to return.*

Despite the initial lift in mood following the Gray's Inn Road to Wapping demonstration, it was becoming increasingly difficult to keep up the levels of morale. Reports had been coming into the Operations Room that some people had not been turning up for their designated picket duties and the number of clerical strikers attending the Wednesday and Saturday evening demonstrations at Wapping had dropped. After a lot of soul searching by the committee members, it was decided that people would be fined (have their strike pay deducted) if they did not show up for their picketing duties. It was also decided that clerical strikers would have to 'clock in' at Wapping on Saturday evenings. The chapel membership accepted the decision and active members of the strike, who were not committee members, were put in charge of overseeing the process.

Helen: *I got involved in organizing the picket rotas and checking that people had turned up. That was murder because people's friends used to lie to me and say 'they have just gone up the road to get a sandwich' and I'd know they just hadn't turned up, but what can you do?*

THE RAGGED TROUSERED CABARET

☆ ☆ ☆ ☆ PRESENT ☆ ☆ ☆ ☆

THE ROYAL WEDDING ALTERNATIVE SHOW

ON THE GREEN AT
WELLCLOSE SQUARE THE HIGHWAY
23rd. JULY WAPPING 4–9 p.m.

ARTISTES INCLUDE

SURFING DAVE · SOGAT SINGERS · P. R. MURRAY · PATRIC CUNNANE · ANTI-APARTHEID SINGERS · LOL WESS (COMPERE · SKINT VIDEO · IAN McPHERSON · PORKY THE POET · MARIA TOLLY · IAN SAVILLE

SURPRISE SPECIAL GUESTS & SPEAKERS
INCLUDING KEN LIVINGSTONE &
☆ ☆ **THE BICYCLE THIEVES** ☆ ☆
PLENTY OF REFRESHMENTS AVAILABLE

18

The Final Offer

Talks between News International and the unions reopened on 22nd August, with scant information filtering back to the strikers, and on Wednesday 27th, a lunchtime demonstration organized by the national union and lead by Brenda Dean and Danny Sergeant, marched from Fleet Street to Wapping. Despite a good turn-out, the column marched straight into Wellclose Square, with no attempt being made to block the road. Both Dean and Sergeant made speeches and both were heckled and booed.

On 1st September, a large turn-out of strikers lobbied delegates at the TUC Conference in support of a motion from the NGA which called for the TUC's General Council instruction that the EETPU inform its members at Wapping that they were engaged in work normally done by other unions, to be reviewed. The motion was carried by a majority of 2 to 1.

There was much euphoria outside the Conference Hall when the result was announced and even Brenda Dean was cheered when she appeared. In reality the result meant very little. The electricians had been scabbing at Wapping for eight months. There was little possibility that they would listen to an instruction from the TUC and, when a decision was finally taken at the end of November, the General Council voted 23 to 21 not to take any further action against the EETPU. On the same day as the General Council decision, *The Guardian* printed a leaked internal memo from News International revealing that the company had reached an agreement with senior EETPU officials in the summer of 1985 over sole bargaining rights (but not union recognition) and pay for their workers at Wapping and Kinning Park.

On the 15th September, news started to reach the strikers that talks had resumed and that an offer was about to be made. Three days later, the SOGAT FOCs and MOCs were called to the union's headquarters at Hadleigh.

John: *I received a phone call from the Branch at 9am, telling me there was going to be a meeting with Brenda Dean to discuss the latest offer from the company and that the ballot papers were already being sent out to the branches for distribution. Brenda expressed little emotion at the meeting and didn't give much detail about the talks. Unfortunately, a lot of the FOCs made long rhetorical speeches, without really putting her on the spot.*

It appeared that, for Brenda, the meeting was just another irritation and that she would be very happy if she never saw us again.

When the ballot form arrived, strikers became aware that there would be no jobs for them, although there was mention of future recruitment: 'no dismissed worker will be excluded from future employment opportunities with relevant News International companies by reason of his/her dismissal'.

The offer did not include any union recognition but, instead, proposed a Joint National Council, with three representatives from News International, two each from the print production unions and one ex-officio representative from the TUC. This Council would only be able to deal with conciliation and communication problems. The idea of a Council had been proposed by the unions during negotiations prior to the strike and again in April, but had been rejected by News International.

Finally, described as 'compensation', there was an increase in the previous total monetary offer, which had been made in May, from £50 million to £55 million. This was mainly because of the withdrawal of the offer of the Gray's Inn Road site which, by this time, the company was in the process of selling to Independent Television News (ITN). This part of the offer included four weeks pay for every year of service, with a maximum of £205 per week and a minimum payment of £2,000.

The letter from Brenda Dean accompanying the ballot form included the following statement: 'we draw your attention to paragraph 1.1 of the offer which is the Company's proposal to us. News International insisted upon including that paragraph, stating that without it there would be no offer at all from them and thus no move from their stance that the previous offer of May was withdrawn and there would be no further negotiations'. Paragraph 1.1 stated that 'this offer would be treated as made to a union only if that union agrees to recommend acceptance of the offer'. This was a fairly spineless way of the union recommending the offer without actually having to use the words.

Within a few days of the offer being announced, the national union finalized a deal with *The Daily Telegraph* which included many of the terms and conditions that the News International workers had taken strike action against. When asked in a television interview why SOGAT had accepted this offer, Bill Miles, a National Officer, said 'we see it as the way forward'. *The Telegraph* deal meant that the strikers' call for involving the rest of Fleet Street in the dispute was becoming less and less attainable.

Despite the continuing isolation, many of those still actively involved in the strike were working to achieve a 'No' vote in the ballot. This did not please Murdoch, who announced that he was going to freeze the offer as he wasn't satisfied with the way that the ballot was being run. Brenda Dean stated that the ballot would continue and Murdoch did not carry out his threat.

As part of the efforts to galvanize support against the offer, the London Machine Branch organized a mass meeting of all strikers, which was held at Westminster Central Hall on the afternoon of the 25th September. There were over 1,000 strikers present and their numbers were swelled by a large contingent of, mainly machine branch members' wives. The event was very effective, but stage managed, and included a speech by a wife whose husband had died during the dispute, calling for a 'No' vote.

On that same evening, the clerical chapels held their own meeting, which was well attended and included many of those who had found work elsewhere and were no longer involved in the strike on a daily basis. Many contributions from the floor called for a rejection of the offer, while only one person spoke in favour.

On 8th October, at around 5pm, the ballot result was announced: SOGAT members rejected the offer by 2,372 votes to 960, which was an even larger majority against than the previous ballot. The NGA strikers also voted against, by 556 to 116, with the engineers voting 'No' by 107 to 47.

John: *When the outcome of the ballot was announced, the mood at the Branch office, where all the FOCs and MOCs had been waiting for the result to come through, was almost euphoric and many were stunned by the result. In addition, the meeting passed a motion to be submitted to the SOGAT London District Council, calling for an escalation of the dispute, including requesting the National Executive to impose a levy of all SOGAT members to support those on strike.*

The ballot result was announced on a Wednesday and that evening the regular demonstration took place at Wapping. Buoyed by the result, the turn-out was larger than usual and the mood was jubilant. Instead of marching from Tower Hill to Wapping, the crowd turned around and marched towards Aldgate. With the police struggling to regroup, it continued down the Mile End Road and fights broke out with the police when TNT lorries, which had been caught in the resulting traffic jams, were set upon by demonstrators. With a residents march taking place near the plant on the same evening, the crowds were large enough to ensure that the distribution of the papers was badly disrupted. Reports on the radio later that evening stated that 13 police had been injured during the demonstration. There was no mention of injuries to the demonstrators.

19

Walkabouts

The day after the ballot result, a breakdown of the voting appeared and, for the striking clerical chapels, it did not make good reading. Of those that voted, 231 rejected the offer and 198 accepted. With these figures, it was becoming even harder for the clerical chapels to have an effect on the direction of the dispute and to keep up the morale of those still involved. A large majority of those who were still active were from the TNL chapel and some felt that the News Group FOC, George Hall, had too much influence when so few of his members were still involved. However, the vast majority of the committee was from TNL and every decision that was taken to the chapels was debated and voted upon. There were occasional disagreements, but this was to be expected in the 'pressure cooker' atmosphere that existed. There could be no questioning George's commitment to the dispute and things must have been very difficult for him and his wife, Carol, who was Deputy MOC of the TNL clerical chapel, as they found themselves deprived of two incomes and the dispute taking up 100% of their lives

Despite the worrying signs thrown up by the ballot, the clerical chapels continued to try and give the dispute impetus and it was at this time that they proposed a different kind of picketing at Wapping. The idea had originally been suggested by a local resident from the Tower Hamlets Print Workers Support Group. The clerical striker who attended the Support Group took the idea to the regular FOCs/MOCs meeting where it was agreed that the 'walkabouts', as they became known, should be tried out on the following Saturday. The tactic involved the usual march to Wapping but, on arrival at Wellclose Square, groups of 20 to 30 strikers, with a local resident as their guide, would walk around pre-planned routes away from The Highway. The police found it difficult to control and, consequently, lorries leaving the plant could not be guaranteed uninterrupted passage.

Graham: *Our presence was quickly noted and two officers on foot began to tail* us. *We spotted them from time to time, lurking down alleyways and side streets, assuming an unconcerned attitude and later, when we stopped at a public loo, they came round a corner and walked right into us. Their embarrassment was acute before they composed themselves and wandered on … whistling! Yes, they really did whistle.*

But as the night wore on, the police presence became more oppressive and a van carrying half a dozen officers took up the surveillance. It was a game of 'cat and mouse' as they did their best to pursue us through the narrow streets and alleys of Wapping, Shadwell and Whitechapel. At one stage, we emerged onto the dual-carriageway at Butcher's Row, having temporarily lost our shadow, in time to see an articulated TNT lorry turn the corner from The Highway. Our noble notion of stopping it by standing, or sitting, in the road, proved naïve as it accelerated towards us. One or two people hurled stones at it as it passed, but the missiles were no more than nuisance value as, by this time, all the lorries had wire mesh screens covering the windows. The stones just bounced back, causing more danger to the throwers than the occupants. Even so, some of us were concerned that a lorry might go out of control and we pressed our colleagues to consider the consequences if it did. But they saw the drivers as mercenaries, which they undoubtedly were, and considered them legitimate targets in a war.

After this and similar incidents involving other print workers, the police considered us a threat and delayed the departure of the lorries. We only saw them occasionally and then much later in the evening. That was considered a victory. The 'walkabouts' continued however, mostly without further incident, for many weeks. Their success in delaying the distribution lorries undoubtedly hingeing on the threat of the earlier violence being repeated. Personally, I had no time for the stone throwing, but one has to admit that, without it, the lorries would have rolled out of the plant unhindered.

As the weeks passed, we attracted even more police attention. Big green buses would pull up and disgorge two or three dozen officers, who either insisted that we split up and forbade us to take certain routes, or merely escorted us, marching in procession on either flank, on our exhaustive tour of the East End.

Back at Commercial Road our group, complete with escort, would be the object of much jealousy from colleagues not considered worthy of such close attention. Finally, at one or two in the morning, we led them back to the plant, where they clambered wearily aboard their buses to three ironic cheers.

Totally alien to our previously normal lives, we found ourselves in a kind of 'twilight zone' on the edge of the law. If you had suggested to any of us, before the dispute began, that we would do the things I have described, our reaction would have been one of disbelief. We didn't much like what we were doing, it was often frightening and we constantly risked arrest, but we took strength from one another.

We weren't kids out for kicks and we didn't have political motives: we were women with children at home, elderly men with bad feet, ordinary people doing extraordinary things because nobody, not our union leadership, the TUC, the Labour Party, our fellow union members, were doing anything meaningful to help us get our jobs, and our lives, back.

Marie: *The 'walkabouts' were quite frightening because we were so vulnerable: turning off into those little side streets, knowing that you could get beaten. I could understand the frustration, because our leadership never went all out to win the dispute. A lot of people were becoming criminalized. I understood why someone would lob a brick at a lorry.*

Frank: *I hope the 'walkabouts' were worthwhile. Simply standing around at Wapping tended to get a bit cold and monotonous, so I found them very enjoyable. We strolled around having a chat. But there is no way of knowing how effective they were, if they really did have any serious effect on the dispute. I would like to think that they did cause some embarrassment. It seems fairly obvious that if you have a couple of van-loads of police following you around, then you must have been causing them a bit of bother. But as to the ultimate end, whether it did cause any real delays, I don't know.*

I don't know who's responsible for those automatic Portaloos, but they lost a hell of a lot of money at Aldgate Bus Station one night. 10p went in the slot and it was 'hold the door open'. Then in-out, in-out as the whole group went in for the one 10p.

20

Clerical Disharmony

As the printing industry expanded in the mid-1800s, the need for additional unskilled labour increased and, by the 1920s, newspapers had become mass circulation publications with large administrative functions attached.

The National Union of Clerks (NUC) represented clerical workers within the newspaper and general printing industries, but a breakaway group organised themselves within a separate Newspaper Clerks Guild and, following a disagreement with the NUC, left to form the London Press Clerks' Association (LPCA).

In July 1920, the LPCA was accepted into membership of The National Society of Operative Printers and Assistants (NATSOPA) and its 1,500 members became the clerical section of the London Branch. Whilst clerical workers continued to be enrolled on a national basis, those in London eventually formed their own branch.

In the following half-century, the London Clerical Branch grew in numbers and organisational strength. By 1982, when NATSOPA amalgamated with SOGAT, the Branch had grown to a membership of 13,000, with three full time officials based at Caxton House in South London and an elected branch committee consisting of union officials from the various workplaces.

On 23rd October 1986, the Autumn delegate meeting of the London Clerical Branch took place. The Branch was facing a crisis, with hundreds of its members at News International having been sacked and the management at other newspapers attempting to impose job losses and inferior working conditions. The situation was not helped by infighting between the branch secretary and his two assistants which led to factions forming amongst the branch committee.

Relations between the clerical strikers on the one hand, and their branch officials and committee on the other, were often strained. This situation, though regrettable, was probably inevitable given that the branch committee members (who were chapel officials in Fleet Street and beyond) and the full time branch officials (who continued to run the London Clerical Branch throughout the dispute) were not themselves on strike. This distinction was a fundamental factor in the on-going conflict between the two groups. The strikers, forced into a corner and living and breathing the strike, with some working every waking moment to pursue it, were sceptical, in some instances perhaps unfairly, about the commitment of the people at Branch level.

The fact that the TNL FOC was a long-standing member of the branch committee, whose loyalties were split between the chapel and the branch, caused some heated debates at chapel meetings when, in the early weeks of the dispute, he reported on decisions concerning the strike taken at Branch level. Several such decisions were overturned, leaving the FOC out on a limb. Such stresses and strains eventually proved too much for him and, to everyone's regret, he dropped out of the dispute due to ill-health.

John: *When we discussed things at the chapel committee meetings, the decisions were always near unanimous. But in the early days, when KB was still FOC, he was torn between the branch and the chapel and it became embarrassing as decisions that he brought from the Branch were rejected by the chapel committee, or at the chapel meetings. His illness, I think, stemmed from his being torn between the two. His departure meant that there were no strikers on the branch committee. There were some individuals who worked hard on our behalf, including union reps who were not members of the Branch committee, but the people who were trying to run it at the Branch were still taking a wage home. They didn't suffer like we did. Some of the branch committee turned up at Wapping when they wanted to and if they were seen once a month, that was considered good enough. But we lived and died it.*

We made our policies in committee and put them to the chapel, so we had every confidence when we took those proposals forward to mass meetings and the like. Everything we did was through the chapel.

Frank: *During all the previous years, when there were just the regular quarterly chapel meetings, there was a kind of 'them and us' situation. The FOC sat on the platform and made his report on what had happened in this or that department and it was all very routine. But once the dispute started, it was a kind of war-time situation, we were all in it together.*

There had always been ordinary chapel members who doubted the motives of their Chapel officials. Were they doing the job out of a deep commitment to the welfare of their fellow workers, or were they just ambitious? Did they have a political axe to grind? Similar reservations were expressed about the Branch officers and the national leadership during the dispute. However, the chapel officials, through their obvious and genuine commitment to the strike and to the strikers, confounded their critics.

Early on in the dispute, one of the first bones of contention was strike pay. The decision on how much the strikers should be given each week from branch funds was taken by the branch committee – all of whom were in full employment – and this was resented by the strikers, who believed such people had little understanding of their situation.

An attempt to secure a levy from all the London Clerical Branch members to support the strikers was not entirely successful. The Branch would not make such a levy compulsory, so it was left to the diligence of each chapel's collectors, and the willingness of individual members, to cough up. Often, a striker would address a chapel meeting to stress the importance of such donations to the survival of those in dispute and a levy of anything between 50p and £2 a week would be agreed. Invariably, attendances at such meetings were poor and the collectors subsequently faced the age-old argument from reluctant members that they had not been at the meeting when the decision was taken, etc, etc. At chapels where it was thought there was little chance that even the members attending a meeting would sanction a levy, a lump-sum payment from chapel funds would be secured. That way, they didn't feel that the money was directly out of their own pockets!

Organizing levies took time and with unemployment benefit withheld, and the unions funds sequestrated, clerical strikers received little or no money during the first few weeks of the dispute. At one particular weekly chapel meeting early on in the dispute, the announcement that there would be no strike pay that week caused dismay and despondency among the hard-pressed strikers and morale was low. Suddenly, right on cue, the FOC from the *Daily Express* materialized waving a cheque; enough money to ensure £5 per head for each striker. He was cheered to the rafters. A hasty telephone call had done the trick.

During those early days, such donations were used to off-set the pitifully low strike pay and six weeks passed before the national union began payments of £12 a week. When regular payments were at last forthcoming from a combination of official national union payments, branch funds and outside donations, they did not approach the levels enjoyed by the members of other, richer branches. On the picket line, machine men expressed the view that they were benefiting from years of high union dues and that if the clericals had paid the same, they too would be getting more. In other words: 'it's your own fault'. They refused to recognize that their higher wages enabled them to pay much larger subscriptions and that clerical dues reflected members' lower pay.

Efforts were made, periodically, to redress the balance in strike pay and Brenda Dean was even persuaded to instigate an inquiry. But as the strike continued, nothing was achieved and the gulf remained.

Although the branch committee would not impose such a policy, attempts were made to dissuade members at other newspapers from handling Murdoch's products. His papers were reaching clerical members in the libraries of all the other newspaper houses, where they were displayed for reading and their stories cut and filed for future reference. Meetings of librarians were called to assess the feasibility of them refusing to handle the papers, but attendances were poor and it was clear that fear of management reprisals ran too deep for them to contemplate taking any action.

The only demonstration at Wapping organized by the clerical branch took place in February, when some 500 clerical members from across Fleet Street joined their striking colleagues and marched to the News International plant. The march was an attempt to stimulate a sense of solidarity between the strikers and those not directly involved in the dispute, introducing them to the intimidating 'Fortress' for the first time and revealing the lengths to which the police were prepared to go to protect the plant and the distribution of the papers.

The idea of holding regular clerical marches was not pursued by the branch, even though they would have increased awareness of, and participation in, the dispute among clerical workers outside the strike.

Traditionally the branch had its own 'employment agency' which placed people into the clerical post vacancies that occurred at the various workplaces. This had served the branch well in the past, giving it some degree of control over the unionised clerical jobs. Consequently, in situations such as the 1979 shut down of *The Times* and *Sunday Times*, many clerical workers were able to find work within other publications. Despite opposition from the TNL/NGN chapel committee when the dispute started, the branch adopted a policy of giving priority to strikers when filling job vacancies or temporary posts in 'The Street'. On the face of it, that was to be commended, but it was a policy with two sides. On the one hand it reduced the amount of money the branch was required to pay out each week in strike pay and gave an increasing number of strikers the opportunity to work and earn a reasonable living again. Those strikers who took jobs at other publications paid £15 per week into the hardship fund to support their non-working colleagues.

The pressure on strikers, especially those with families, to take a job as the dispute lengthened into months, was immense. But employment distanced those in work from the struggle. Back in the security of a steady job, where the strike was met with indifference, or even outright hostility, by their new colleagues; where they earned good money which enabled them to pick up the pieces of their lives, they were a long way from the harsh realities of the picket line and they found it harder and harder to summon the will to go down to Wapping on a cold Saturday night, even though they knew their friends were still there. Commitment was undermined and, in some cases, people abandoned the strike altogether. The branch was seen as actively encouraging this situation and the inevitable question was asked: 'does the branch think this strike is winnable?'

Pam: *I did some temp work during the dispute and found there was almost total apathy. If all our people had worked a fortnight back in The Street, the strike would have been over in two months. People would have given up if they had seen the apathy. There was hardly anyone at the* Daily Telegraph *who had any sympathy with us. They sat there reading* The Sun, *it was incredible. They lived in their own little world and the strike had nothing to do with them. They paid the levy and thought they were doing their bit. And some of them even disagreed with that. SOGAT members may have been guilty of something similar during the miners' strike, and we were the only chapel in Fleet Street to have a levy for them. The only chapel!*

The Autumn delegate meeting was attended by chapel representatives from all the national newspapers, as well as organizations such as Reuters and the Press Association. The agenda was dominated by the News International dispute and revealed that the Branch had, to date, spent over half a million pounds pursuing its campaign.

On the morning of the meeting, branch officers attended a TNL/NGN chapel committee meeting in an attempt to persuade them to withdraw their emergency motion in favour of its own. The proposal was rejected.

The chapel committee motion called for maximum support for the demonstrations at Wapping and for strikers to be regularly invited to address chapel meetings. It also called for as much financial support as possible from other chapels, but stopped short of asking for a levy to be imposed.

But the final three parts of the motion were the most contentious. The first of these demanded that Murdoch's products be boycotted at all unionised printing houses. The second, that every effort be made to obtain a 24 hour shutdown of Fleet Street, as quickly as possible, to achieve maximum solidarity. Finally, it insisted that chapel officers be part of the negotiating team in all future negotiations with News International.

Graham: *The motion was moved powerfully by George Hall, but opposed by the branch committee on the grounds that the call for a 24 hour shutdown of Fleet Street was unattainable. Assistant branch secretary, Barry Fitzpatrick, delivered a fine and very emotional speech which stressed how much the strikers had sacrificed over the past months on behalf of all Fleet Street workers and said that any request from them ought to be met. Then he spoilt it all by saying that this one was the exception.*

The old bickering between the TNL/NGN chapel officials and the branch officers surfaced yet again. (Oh, how we all wish that these differences could have been laid aside). But the debate was salvaged by some eloquent contributions from our members, notably Karen Tomkins and Michele Martin, and the motion was carried overwhelmingly.

Although the motion would now become Branch policy, the strikers were still mainly reliant on those who opposed it, to carry out its implementation.

Graham: *In October, the chapel administration came up with one or two ideas to breathe some new life into the strike. One was that the chapel should produce its own newsletter to express the views, not of the administration, but of the rank and file members. A volunteer was called for to edit the sheet and as I didn't hold any office, and was probably the only applicant, they gave me the job.*

Titled Hard Times, *the first edition appeared in November and was distributed to members at chapel meetings and handed out at demonstrations to anyone who would take a copy. The lead story criticized the chapel officials for failing to organize a chapel meeting immediately members received a letter from the company offering them compensation if they deserted the strike. Stressing the* point that many felt intimidated by the individual approach and needed the reassurance that a meeting with their colleagues would bring, it lamented the failure to convene such a meeting in time to prevent the wobblers, in their isolation, from accepting the offer. Many people who took the money subsequently regretted their lack of resolve and felt a deep remorse.

Over the next few days, people were telling me that the branch secretary was 'ranting and raving' about the article. I only had a nodding acquaintance with the man, but resolved to see him and clear the air.

Notwithstanding the rumours, I was taken aback by his reaction. He launched into a tirade, saying he'd had enough of the constant criticism levelled at himself and his fellow officers by the chapel administration and that it was clear that this latest blast emanated from the same source. He accused me, personally, of being a member of the Socialist Workers Party, as he believed the piece had all the hallmarks of their style.

When, at last, I was able to get a word in (and trying hard to remain composed under the onslaught) I told him that he had misunderstood the purpose of the newsletter; that it was not expounding the views of the chapel administration, but those of ordinary chapel members, and although critical of the stance taken by the branch over the proposed action in Fleet Street, it had also criticized both branch and chapel officers over their bickering.

As for the SWP, I told him I was a proud Labour-Party voter who had never been a member of any political party and that I considered the piece, though forthright, far removed from their inflammatory style. I was probably more offended by this comparison than with any other of the accusations levelled at me.

He was obviously under immense pressure and overwhelmed by criticism. Perhaps it was the last straw. His reaction, however, seemed to me totally irrational. I recount it merely to illustrate the magnitude of the rift that had developed between branch and chapel and reiterate, as I did at the time, that the fault was not all on one side.

21

The Individual Offers

On the 31ˢᵗ October, Murdoch sent a letter to all the strikers, announcing that 'we are prepared to offer directly to each employee dismissed as a result of the strike, a termination payment calculated in the way set out in our last offer'.

The offer, which was a blatant attempt to undermine the recent ballot result, would remain open until 10ᵗʰ November and the letter boasted that '*The News of the World* is two million copies ahead of its nearest rival. *The Sun* leads its competition by 900,000 and both *The Times* and *Sunday Times* are enjoying huge increases in advertising and pagination'. Murdoch concluded that 'the strike is doing no good to anyone. Indeed its futility must be evident to all'.

The national union, aware that the company was about to offer compensation on an individual basis, responded with a letter to strikers on the same day, urging them not to accept. The letter also informed people that, since the ballot result, efforts had been made to raise further support for the strike from within SOGAT and the wider trade union movement. Finally, strikers were invited to a mass meeting at Westminster Central Hall on the 10ᵗʰ November.

For the clerical strikers who were still active in the strike, there was real concern that those who had voted against in the recent ballot, or had not voted at all, would be tempted by the offer. Some members wanted a chapel meeting called straightaway, but it was three days before the chapel committees met and a further two days before all chapel members received a letter from the joint chapels.

The letter asked people to show solidarity by returning the forms to the chapels, in order that they could be sent back to Murdoch at Wapping, and members were invited to a meeting at Caxton House on the morning of Friday 7ᵗʰ November. This weekday morning time slot meant that many of those who were now working could not attend.

John: *Only once did the committee have a serious disagreement: it was at the time of the individual offers. We wanted people to turn the offers down, but we had a duty to spell out what that would mean to them in the way of more effort and further hardship. Only then could we explain what we had to offer in return, which was to get the rest of Fleet Street involved and press for a proper, democratically elected strike committee, instead of the old regime of FOCs (some of whom were to end up taking the money). It was felt that, if we were too open, we would lose a lot of people. But I, among others, refused to consider anything less. We weren't prepared to con people. We left it for four days before calling a meeting and were honest about the situation, while calling on everyone to stay loyal to the strike. But it was too late. By the time we got round to the meeting, most people had made their minds up and some had already applied to the company for the money. We should have held the meeting the day after the offers went out. Some people were very upset over being criticised about it, but it was one of the few mistakes we made throughout the whole dispute and, over a full year, that's not a bad record.*

The clerical chapel meeting was well attended, and the presence of the two assistant branch secretaries, urging people not to accept the individual offer, helped heal some of the recent rifts between the branch and the chapels. Although the meeting was a positive one, committee members had already been receiving calls from individuals, some of whom were wavering, and others who had already accepted the offer.

John: *I had a phone call from Charlie T. He was really distressed. He told me he'd signed the letter from Murdoch and that he was now 'totally worthless'. After the effort he had put in over the previous 10 months, it came like a bolt out of the blue.*

   Mick: *It wasn't that they scabbed. But a lot of them hadn't really involved themselves in the dispute and they took the money. As they saw it, they weren't going to get their jobs back, so they had nothing to continue for. But they lessened our chances by taking the money and I haven't got any time for them anymore. I met PF and he was saying that the union owed him a living and he should have his membership card back. I asked him why he'd ripped it up, because that's what he did when he took the money. But I just can't be bothered any more. I'm tired of them and I don't want to know them. I could never socialise with them like I used to because it could never be the same. I might acknowledge them, but that would be all.*

The following week, Murdoch wrote to all the strikers again, extending the individual offer until the 24th November. He stated that

148

'to date, News International have had more than 1,500 acceptances and compensation has been paid to many of these. Those who have applied include at least six FOCs, a number of chapel chairmen and many chapel committee members'. He went on 'letters continue to arrive from people who are keen to accept'.

However, at the same time, the conciliation service ACAS, who were required by the Employment Protection Act to explain the offer to individuals, reported the real figures, which showed that 900 had accepted the offer and that there had been an additional 300 enquiries. Nevertheless, the striking clerical members could not help but see that attendances at chapel meetings, and at the demonstrations at Wapping, were on the decline.

Denise: *When individuals were offered the money, it was the beginning of the end. People were divided and, though it didn't seem that there were that many taking the money, gradually the numbers crept up and I think people lost heart. The papers were giving a daily figure of people accepting the offer and it became demoralising. But he (Murdoch) never had enough. It wasn't as though we were completely disintegrating.*

22

The National Levy

Despite the fact that around 20% had accepted the individual offer, over 2,000 strikers attended a mass meeting at Westminster Central Hall on the evening of 10th November. Brenda Dean gave a report which mentioned, but did not criticise, comments made by Norman Willis two days earlier: the TUC General Secretary had stated that the unions should compromise and accept that the electricians and TNT drivers should be allowed to continue working at Wapping. He also suggested that the national unions should, if necessary, override the wishes of their members in order to obtain a settlement.

The meeting was very calm compared to previous gatherings and some of the leading figures in the dispute, such as Michael Hicks and Tony Issacs, went out of their way to be supportive of Brenda Dean. This appeared to be a tactical decision, as there was a constant fear that the national union could call off the strike at any time, and they needed to keep her on side. Also, much depended on her helping to deliver a 'Yes' vote for the forthcoming national levy and this topic dominated her report: she gave details of plans to call on all members, nationwide, to support the News International strikers.

The London District Council had called for the national levy of SOGAT members following the rejection of Murdoch's second offer. The National Executive had met with all of the Branch Secretaries from around the country at a meeting in London on 20th October and, on the following day, the FOCs and MOCs were addressed by Brenda Dean at their regular Tuesday meeting.

She reported that there had been a poor response to the idea from most of the branches and the National Executive had decided to ballot the membership on the introduction of a levy of 58p a week, rather than impose it, as they were entitled to do under the union's general rules. She stated that there would be a special edition of the SOGAT Journal devoted to the levy and that an executive member, possibly (after representations from the FOCs) accompanied by a striker, would address each branch throughout the country. With a timescale of around six weeks to visit 70 different branches, there was a certain amount of scepticism about whether this could be achieved. After two weeks of campaigning, Brenda Dean reported that just four branches had been visited. The special edition of the SOGAT journal appeared in November and her contribution, under the title 'Help To Save the Union We All Love and Need', spelt out the financial crisis faced by SOGAT:

> 'The brutal truth is that the union is financially crippled … What has happened is that the sequestration and legal costs which we have faced as a result of the News International dispute, have slashed the total assets of the union in half … If Rupert Murdoch pursues us in the courts, as he had indicated he will, and as he can under the current state of the law, then he will bankrupt SOGAT.'

She went on to explain that the Executive decided to ballot the entire membership, rather than impose the levy, because they believed that the crisis involved everyone. She said that a 'Yes' vote would be 'helping to demonstrate to the management of News International that SOGAT and our members are not an easy pushover'. She concluded by apologizing for asking for the 58p:

> 'Colleagues, it distresses me deeply to have to make this appeal. For half of my short period of eighteen months in office as General Secretary we have been involved in this dispute, the most bitter in the history of SOGAT. It is physically and emotionally draining. It has diverted my energies away from the introduction of improved services to you, our members, and the need to modernize and see the union better managed. And coming from the provinces myself, I know that the levy the union seeks is money hard-earned in areas where there are few easy pickings.'

The whole tenor of the piece was unassertive, pleading with the members to save the union from bankruptcy brought about by the News International dispute. Whether by design, or a failure to communicate, she failed to convey a full-blooded, whole-hearted support for the strike and readers could have been forgiven for concluding that the remedy was not to contribute to a levy, thereby hastening the end of a strike that was depleting their union's resources and seriously affecting the benefits that they themselves should have been enjoying.

The journal also contained messages of support from musicians and actors such as Pete Townsend and Glenda Jackson, and around a dozen articles by various branch secretaries from different parts of the country. Many strikers felt it would have been beneficial to have seen a statement signed by all the branch secretaries, calling for a 'Yes' vote and full support for the strikers. The contribution from the London Clerical Branch secretary, Chris Robbins, did just that and was in marked contrast to Brenda Dean's effort:

> 'If you don't vote for the levy you will be giving not only Rupert Murdoch, but all employers in the printing and publishing industry their best Christmas present in years.
>
> The cleaners, secretaries, machine operators, drivers and others who make up the workforce of News International have been through the longest and bitterest dispute in our history to win back what most of us have – a job and recognition of our union.
>
> The cost has been almost incalculable, both to the individual members and the national union, but we have survived through the difficulties of the past ten months. We all have to support the courage of our members in the News International dispute for turning down a redundancy package in the full knowledge that in doing so they committed themselves to many more months of severe financial hardship and a hard winter. Since the beginning of the dispute the chapels and branches in London have raised over £2 million through voluntary levies, benefits and other fundraising activities. By any standards, this is a magnificent response to our members in dispute. In addition to this, branches all over the country have given sizeable contributions.
>
> But it is clear that if we are to continue the dispute and survive as a union, then all members of SOGAT will have to participate in sharing the financial burden. Victory, or defeat, may well decide the future of our members not only in national newspapers, but in many other sectors of the industry.
>
> A levy of all of us in SOGAT will be a small price to pay for the courage of our members who have chosen not to be bought off – and a small price to pay to ensure that the national union has the financial stability to protect and defend all its members, in every part of the printing industry.'

One contribution which, in hindsight, forewarned of the final outcome of the national levy was written by Frank Neal, branch secretary of the East Anglia region. He described how his branch had previously written to every member asking them to contribute 10p a week until the dispute had been resolved.

> 'Unfortunately, with just a few exceptions, this cry for help for the national union fell on deaf ears. Why, I asked myself, had so few people responded? Are we asking for too much, or would it create hardship amongst the membership? The answer to each of those questions was a most definite no, so the answer must lie elsewhere.

Until the amalgamation with NATSOPA, we had never had any involvement with the production of newspapers and many of the members employed in general print do honestly believe that the members in national newspapers are grossly overpaid and over manned, when comparisons are made with themselves. They think they are a group of inflexible workers who are reluctant to accept change and the problems they are now facing with Murdoch have been brought about by their intransigent attitude ... They appear to be completely complacent and utterly apathetic as to what is happening to our society and to the ex-employees of News International. They are completely convinced that what happened to those members cannot happen to them! They couldn't be more wrong.'

The failure to deliver the promised branch meetings, which would have helped to change these attitudes, convinced many of the strike activists that the levy would not be supported and, sure enough, the East Anglian experience was repeated nationally. The result, announced on 13th January, was 44,267 in favour and 51,187 against, with a 56% turnout. It was one of the final nails in the dispute's coffin, but there was little doubt that a real campaign would have swayed the vote. Instead, Manchester Central and the Scottish Graphical branches were the only ones outside the London area to vote in favour. Even in London the turn-out was poor, with the clerical branch voting three to one in favour with only 44% voting.
Commenting on the result Brenda Dean said:

'It is perhaps a further example of the North-South divide. Down here we do not always appreciate the hardships our members have been enduring. There have been many redundancies and other cuts to retain printing capacity and, to many SOGAT members, 58p a week is a big sum to find.'

The reaction of the clerical news sheet *Hard Times* was less philosophical. Under the heading 'Betrayed', it commented:

'How can the 51,187 SOGAT members who voted against the levy justify their actions? It's one thing to refuse to black Murdoch's titles when jobs may be at stake – though that decision was fundamental in prolonging the dispute – but to reject a call to donate 58p a week out of your wage packet, to sustain the union and the strike, is indefensible.

Brenda Dean said that the result was 'perhaps a further example of North-South divide ... to many SOGAT members 58p a week is a big sum to find'. Surely, members suffering genuine hardship themselves would not have been expected to pay. An issue as important as this should have over-ridden any old animosity about 'fat cats' in the South. We gave generously to the miners and it goes without saying that we would have done the same had it been SOGAT members in dispute. We have been betrayed.'

Joyce: *I have to say this: Londoners think they are better than everybody else. You got it in the dispute. You had certain individuals, 'Jack the Lads', who epitomized that attitude and that's why we lost the ballot for the levy.*

You go up to Peterborough or somewhere, house prices are going up because people are moving out there from London. But there are people in those places who are earning, gross, barely £100 a week, so what is their attitude when they see someone in London getting more than that for a Saturday night. It's hopeless. I know the argument's been that the leadership wasn't there, but Brenda was on a hiding to nothing to convince people like that. You can't, when you're getting a doing at last, suddenly scream help and expect the support of all those people.

23

Prison

Michael Hicks was imprisoned in early December and, though his case received quite a lot of publicity, he was not the fist print worker to be given a custodial sentence in connection with the dispute. In October, David Payne, a Southwark Councilor and member of the SOGAT London Machine Branch, and Robert Tetaur, a sacked *Times* Copy Reader, were sentenced to six months apiece. Stephen Savage, a member of the SOGAT casuals strike committee, was sentenced to three months.

The Payne and Tetaur cases were linked. The incident leading to their convictions arose when Payne was ferrying supplies to the SOGAT van at Wapping, where he came across Tetaur and a TNT driver having a difference of opinion. Payne's car was stacked with bread rolls, sausages and kitchen equipment and, in the court case, both were accused with causing actual bodily harm, with a saucepan cited in evidence as an offensive weapon.

The jail sentence deprived Payne not only of his liberty, but also of the chance to pursue his political career: a Councillor receiving a prison sentence of over three months is automatically banned from holding office for five years, with no right of appeal.

After successfully appealing against their six month sentences, Payne and Tetaur were freed on 24th November, the three appeal judges concluding that the violence may not have been all on one side and that the sentences were longer than necessary. Bob Tetaur said, 'I've never been political. I'm just fighting for my family, my wife Christine and our baby. I'll be back at Wapping. If they'd tried to stop me as a condition of my release I'd have served the full six months sentence'.

Stephen Savage was arrested after a picket at a John Menzies distribution depot in Southend. An affray started after three pickets entered the depot. According to one of those present, Savage was not part of the original struggle, only getting involved when he saw people on the ground getting hurt and needing help. He was subsequently charged with assault on a police officer and was told that he could get a non-custodial sentence if he pleaded guilty. He so pleaded and was sentenced to three months

Michael Hicks had been found guilty of actual bodily harm and sentenced to 12 months imprisonment with eight months suspended. Hicks allegedly pushed a megaphone into a police inspectors face during one of the regular demonstrations at Wapping.

The SOGAT National Executive did not mount any campaign to secure his release and in her autobiography Brenda Dean says of Hicks that he 'wanted to be a martyr and did succeed in getting himself arrested and subsequently sent to jail. Although it was a relief to me to know where he was for a while and that he was beyond making mischief'.

John: *I got on well with Michael Hicks although we had disagreements about how to take the dispute forward and the role of the Communist Campaign Group. However, for a lot of people he was seen as somebody who was always present at Wapping and he filled a void that was left by the union leadership. I had no doubts that his imprisonment was political. A few days after he was jailed I was at one of the regular demonstrations at Wapping and I managed to get hold of the megaphone and address the crowd. I made my feelings clear that we were not going to get Michael Hicks out of prison by marching to Wapping. Instead, I suggested we call the whole of Fleet Street out on strike and march to Brixton prison where he was being held.*

Michael's appeal against his sentence was rejected in January and by the time he was released, the dispute was over.

The feeling among strikers was that custodial sentences would now be the order of the day in an attempt to break their resolve. But the threat of imprisonment did not deter people from picketing and David Payne subsequently spoke at Wapping on many occasions, calling for an escalation of the dispute.

As the year drew to a close, News International turned their attention to putting pressure on the national union to take disciplinary action against their own members. This followed four separate 'taking the gate' incidents at Wapping during the course of December. The company had sent video footage to the unions, who responded by asking the branches to supply volunteers to come forward to admit their part in the incidents. This merely increased the animosity of many of the strikers towards their own union.

24

Michael Delaney

With the arrival of the New Year attention turned towards 24th January and the anniversary of the dispute. However, before then tragedy struck.

John: *It was my second visit to Wapping that day, 10th January. Earlier, in the afternoon, about 300 of us had gathered at St George's Church. We moved out onto The Highway and into Pennington Street, running towards the main gates. The security people just managed to get them shut in time. We spent an hour and a half there before the police amassed enough numbers to push us back onto The Highway. I went back in the evening with my wife for the regular march from Tower Hill. It was very cold, but our spirits were high as we talked about our 'taking the gate' that afternoon. The march and the picketing were fairly uneventful and at about 11.30pm we decided to have an early night and left for home.*

As we drove down the Commercial Road, a TNT lorry passed us going in the opposite direction and we remarked on how unusual it was that it didn't have a police escort. Then, at Butcher's Row, we saw several police cars, a stationary TNT lorry and several people standing in the road. We stopped and went over to see what was happening.

A young lad was lying in the road with a couple of traffic policemen kneeling over him. He was covered by one of their fluorescent jackets, which offered scant protection against the cold. Three other teenage boys were crying hysterically and one kept yelling, 'they've fucking run him over'. We tried to comfort them. In between their sobs, we learned that they'd been crossing the road when the first of two lorries waiting at the traffic lights had moved forward. The three reached the pavement and turned to see their friend, Michael Delaney, crushed under its back wheels. The other lorry, the one we had seen in Commercial Road, had been allowed to continue its journey by the police escort. Michael, who was not connected to the strike, had been out celebrating his 19th birthday.

By this time, several more pickets had arrived and emotions began to run high as they found out what had happened. People were shouting at the police, 'you knew this would happen one day'. I took off my overcoat and offered to cover the lad, only to be told by a Sergeant to 'piss off out of it'. Another picket took exception to this remark and was promptly arrested. Meanwhile, the lorry driver sat in his cab, regularly checking his watch and appearing more concerned about being late delivering Murdoch's papers than about the boy lying in the road.

The ambulance seemed to be taking an eternity to arrive. I kept looking at Michael Delaney and I could see the life draining away from him. I felt totally helpless. What seemed like long periods of silence were shattered by the shouts of the pickets, frustrated by their own impotence and venting their anger on the TNT driver, the police and the ambulance that didn't come. It finally arrived after about 15 minutes and the boy was lifted gently onto a stretcher and driven away.

The police forced the 30 or so pickets back onto the pavement and the lorry, with its customary escort, went on its way. It would have been easy to believe that nothing out of the ordinary had happened, except that Michael Delaney's friend was still shouting, 'they've run him over, they've fucking run him over'.

We were both devastated and could hardly speak on the way home. When we got in, I turned on the local radio to see if there was any news concerning the accident. There was no mention. I decided to ring a phone-in programme and tell them what had happened and the presenter allowed me to speak, virtually uninterrupted, for two or three minutes. I laid the blame firmly at Murdoch's door.

We didn't get much sleep and first thing the next morning I phoned the London Hospital in Whitechapel. They wouldn't give me any details about Michael so, reluctantly, we drove to Leman Street Police Station. As much as we loathed having to deal with the police, we had to know how he was. They told us that Michael Delaney had died at 5 o'clock that morning. Despite not knowing him, or anything about him, we were shattered by the news.

Michael and his family had lived in Tower Hamlets for many years before moving to Seven Kings in Essex and, following his death, the Tower Hamlets Trades Council and the local Print Support Group carried out many initiatives in protest at the way he died and in support of his family, gathering signatures for petitions, lobbying the Home Office and raising money.

A sympathetic lawyer who had assisted many strikers and Wapping residents during the dispute, was employed to represent the family and, in April, an inquest jury returned a majority verdict of unlawful killing, despite the Coroner's recommendation to return a verdict of accidental death. Nevertheless, the Director of Public Prosecutions refused to take any action against the lorry driver and TNT, which made a mockery of the jury system.

Efforts were increased to raise the profile of the campaign and Michael's father, Dick, became a regular at the local support group meetings. A demonstration from Butcher's Row to Wapping was held in September, with Michael's friends and family, Wapping residents, strikers and members of support groups from Oxford and Leicester taking part.

The cost of a private prosecution ran into many thousands of pounds and despite the efforts of the family and their supporters, the amount of money required was never reached. In January 1989, Michael's father was also knocked down by a car and killed.

25

Support Groups

Print Workers' Support Groups played a vital role in assisting the strikers and numbered over 50 at the height of the dispute. During the 1984-85 Miners' strike, countrywide support groups had been formed and many of these were to reform on behalf of the print workers. They ensured that information reached their area and that support for the strikers was maintained. They organized public meetings and raised funds and, often linking with other such groups in their locality, picketed sites connected with News International. Although most of the groups were made up of rank and file activists, some took a more official form, being linked to their local Trades Council, and such direct contact often prompted wider trade union activity.

It was not always easy to persuade strikers to attend groups, even when they were near their own homes but, without this participation, the vital communication between strikers and their supporters was weakened. It was a source of much frustration to some groups, and much embarrassment to active strikers, that supporters were collecting money for the strikers on the streets without one striker from that area taking part.

This situation reflected the conservatism of many of the print workers: in the same way as the national union didn't encourage non-strikers on the picket line in the early days of the dispute, so some strikers did not want to fraternize with 'outsiders' who they saw as interfering in their dispute. Others found that they had enough to cope with fulfilling what was already expected of them in the way of picketing, demonstrating and other duties, and some were simply unable to overcome their shyness. There were, however, strikers who actively participated in their local group, and even those who did not came to recognize the valuable role they played.

Some groups suffered the political sectarianism that plagues the Labour Movement. In Hackney, for example, Communist Party members of the local group refused to accept any criticism of the role some of their (non-striking) colleagues were playing in the dispute and, in Tower Hamlets, the Socialist Workers Party withdrew from the local group within a few weeks of its inauguration, when it became apparent that they would not be able to control it.

The clerical chapel had particularly close links with the Tower Hamlets group: Wapping came within the London Borough of Tower Hamlets and following a meeting organized by the local Trades Council, a Support Group was formed.

John: *The strike had only been on a couple of days when I spoke at my first meeting, which had been called by the Tower Hamlets Trades Council, and it was agreed that a Print Workers' Support Group should be formed. About 50 people crammed into the living room of a house in Cable Street, close to the Wapping plant, for the first meeting and, after the early departure of the SWP, about 30 activists were left. This group gave continued support throughout the strike and linked with local tenants under the banner 'Reclaim Our Streets' to protest against the excessive policing of the dispute and its impact on local residents.*

One of the groups that regularly attended demonstrations at Wapping was the London-based Lesbian and Gay Print Workers Support Group (L&GPSG). Early on during the dispute two members of the L&GPSG were invited to address a clerical chapel meeting at the TUC headquarters at Congress House. They made their way to the podium in the large hall to the accompaniment of some nervous tittering and shuffling of feet. But, with notable dignity, the speakers explained why they supported the strike and how they faced similar problems of non-acceptability, victimization and police harassment. Their departure from the platform, in marked contrast to the excruciating entrance, was marked by a standing ovation

There had been arguments amongst politically active lesbians and gays about whether the print workers should be supported at all because of 'gay bashing' by papers like *The Sun*, but the view that any workers involved in struggle should be supported won the day and the group continued.

The print workers, of course, had no say in the content of the newspapers for which they worked but a 'Right of Reply' campaign, predominantly run by members of the NGA, did exist at *The Sun*. During the miners' dispute, the paper tried to publish a vitriolic attack on miners' leader, Arthur Scargill. The front page story was accompanied by a picture of Scargill with his arm raised, similar to a

Nazi salute, and the headline 'Mine Fuhrer'. Following pressure from the unions, a right of reply was given and the front-page headline was replaced by a statement from the management that the production chapels had refused to print the picture or the headline.

Requests for speakers and literature concerning the strike were originally handled by the Operations Room but, as the workload increased and support groups began to spring up, the London District Council of SOGAT decided to form a body to liaise between the groups and the strikers. The support group co-ordinating team was set up after seven weeks in dispute, originally with two full-time union officials working with a striking clerical member. But the officials quickly returned to their own duties, leaving the clerical member appealing to other strikers to help manage what was already a massive job.

The team functioned with little interference from union bureaucracy. As well as dealing with requests for speakers, it encouraged the formation of new groups and supplied information, literature and strike paraphernalia to existing groups, trade union branches, outside organizations and individuals. Requests for speakers often emptied the pool of people available. Women speakers were in constant demand and the burden was carried mostly by those in the clerical chapel. Indeed, 75% of the speakers in the pool were clerical members and some found themselves addressing two, or even three, meetings in a day. Continuing the demarcation lines that had existed at work, the NGA and SOGAT London Machine Branch insisted on supplying their own speakers for its own contacts, rather than allowing the whole operation to be centrally controlled. But a large number of requests came through the co-ordinating team and individual members of the NGA and machine branch met requests to cover meetings.

In late October, a meeting of all the support groups was called by Tower Hamlets and the co-ordinating team, with the aim of regularizing the groups' activities and discussing the current state of both the groups and the dispute itself. The meeting was attended mainly by the London groups, although there were also delegates from Oxford, Leicester, Essex and Kent, and it was proposed that a national support groups' demonstration should take place at Wapping.

News of the meeting was met with a distinct lack of enthusiasm by Branch and national union officials, who saw it as interference by outsiders. The groups were asking serious questions about the direction the dispute was taking, and attempts were made to undermine the planned march.

All the Saturday evening demonstrations were planned several weeks in advance, and a co-ordinating team member had attended the regular strike committee meeting which confirmed that the 13th December march would be led by the National Support Groups. Then, a couple of weeks after this confirmation, two further marches were announced for the same evening: the support groups would set off from Aldgate East tube station; a march led by the Laison Committee for the Defence of Trade Unions (LCDTU) would march from Tower Hill, and a Women's March from Butcher's Row. There was a heated row at the FOCs/MOCs meeting about this decision as it was felt that there was a deliberate attempt to undermine the support groups' march.

Because of all the planning and hard work that had already taken place, and because of the principle involved, it was decided that the support group march should go ahead regardless of its relegation and, on 13th December, a 'feeder' march of South London support groups crossed London Bridge and joined the main demonstration at Aldgate East. Around 1,000 people then set off down the Commercial Road, where they met the Women's March coming from the opposite direction. The police, obviously confused by three different demonstrations on the same night, decided that the support groups march appeared to be the most vociferous and made several unsuccessful attempts to push it over to one side of the street. But, continuing into The Highway, it blocked the Wapping Lane exit from the plant for over an hour and the marchers, with their banners proclaiming groups from all over the country, received an enthusiastic welcome when they finally reached the main picket at Virginia Street.

In December, the co-ordinating team were approached by a group of musicians, collectively named Test Department. Apart from one or two of the younger, more musically aware members, nobody had ever heard of them! But they said they wanted to play a benefit concert to commemorate the first anniversary of the strike, which would feature a special set based on the printing industry. They would require film, as they used images on a huge screen, the taped sounds of a printing machine room and a venue close to the News International plant that could hold 1,000 people.

Although many were sceptical that the band would be able to fill such a large theatre, the Hackney Empire was chosen for the concert and, over the following weeks, they rehearsed at a studio in Southwark. It soon became obvious, however, that they were running out of money and the co-ordinating team set about writing to different unions asking them to sponsor the event: The National Association of Local Government Officers (NALGO) in Hackney immediately contributed the £600 needed for the hire of the theatre. The band produced its own advertising poster for 'The Siege of Wapping' and the clerical strikers were out fly-posting, as well as attending rehearsals for their own contribution to the proceedings.

On the night, to everyone's delight, it was realized that Test Department enjoyed a cult following which filled the Empire to bursting point.

Clerical strikers, some of whom were members of the SOGAT Singers, took part in the first session and, during the interval, ex-dockworkers' leader, Jack Dash, made a fundraising speech. The band, with its 'industrial' sound created with oil drums and metal tubing, performed a stunning set, aided by the film and audio tapes they had requested (a crew having been smuggled into the machine room at *The Daily Express*) and, by the end of the evening, several thousand pounds had been raised for the strike Hardship Fund.

WAPPING

MARCH & RALLY

STRIKE ANNIVERSARY
a year of struggle

SATURDAY 24th JANUARY

Assemble: Arundel Street, Temple Tube 4pm
Rally: Wellclose Street E1 6.30 pm

National speakers ◆ Music ◆ Special guests ◆ Stalls ◆

SUPPORT THE 5,500 SACKED
BY RUPERT MURDOCH

PRINTWO
FAMI

100'S OF KIDS AT
RISK OF POVERTY

TERRY FRENCH
Betteshanger — 5 years jail

THE
WORLD

SOGAT ■ NGA ■ AEU ■ NUJ

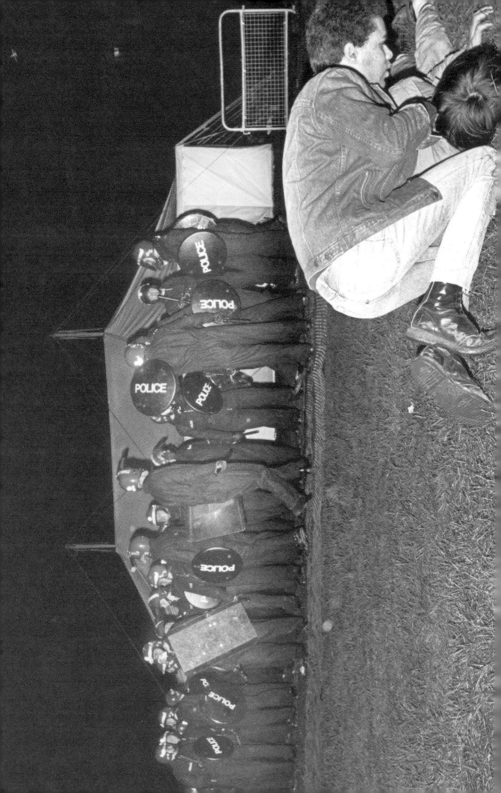

26

The Anniversary and Violence

With the negative result of the ballot for the National Levy having been announced on 13th January, there was a real fear that the number of people attending the planned anniversary demonstration on the 24th would be affected.

The national union had made it clear in early January that the demonstration was for 'rallying purposes only'. They were fearful that any other type of announcement could be construed as encouraging people to break any one of the number of conditions regarding demonstrating at Wapping that had been imposed by the courts and thus face the risk of going back into sequestration.

John: *The national union tried to short-circuit the demonstration on 24th January. They didn't contact people about it and failed to get leaflets and posters out. It was left to the London branches and individuals who broke their backs to get it done. I think they were hoping there would be a very poor turn-out and they could say, 'look, you haven't got any support'. In the end, there was a big turn-out, but there was some violence and they used that as an excuse to end it prematurely.*

Pam: *I was in the Ops Room and people were ringing up saying, 'what the hell's going on, I thought you wanted our support. I've people ready to come up on Saturday and now we are told to keep out'. The miners were told to keep away, but they came anyway.*

On the afternoon of Saturday 24th January 1987, demonstrators began gathering at Arundel Street, adjacent to Temple tube station. They were assembling to march to Wapping in support of the sacked workers, who had now been on strike for exactly a year. Numbers vary regarding how many eventually attended on the day, but those who regularly went to Wapping and had been on some of the bigger demonstrations during the previous year, estimated that this was by far the largest with over 20,000 people present.

The march wound its way from Temple to Fleet Street, where members of the print unions were preparing for their evening's work.

A demonstrator lying injured on the green opposite the Wapping plant (24/1/87). (David Hoffman Photo Library)

The policy of not involving the rest of Fleet Street in the dispute remained unaltered. Consequently, whilst their striking colleagues and their supporters (some of whom had travelled many miles to be there) marched towards Wapping, SOGAT and NGA members remained at work. Later that same evening, they would print the Sunday papers with their accounts of the violence.

The march was a good natured affair but, as they reached The Highway, the demonstrators became aware of a massive police presence. At Wellclose Square a covered stage, complete with a public address system and lighting, and a marquee with notices on its entrances stating 'Speakers and Officials only', had been erected and as the front of the march reached the Square, a band started to play.

With so many people on the march, efforts were made by some of the strikers, including clerical members, to persuade demonstrators to carry on walking up towards Wapping Lane. Unfortunately, as many marchers were not regulars at the demonstrations, the bright lights of the square seemed more inviting, and the few hundred who did go on to Wapping Lane found themselves confronted by three lines of police. At around 7.30pm, Brenda Dean began speaking from the stage and sections of the crowd were chanting 'Off, Off, Off'.

At this point, the police made their first foray into the crowd at the top of Virginia Street, sending in snatch squads with riot shields and helmets.

John: *We had been to Wapping Lane, but there were not enough of us to block the exit and there were lines of police on foot and mounted officers. Walking back along The Highway, we encountered the Special Patrol Group in their vans, flying about at speed and being very intimidating. As we got closer to Wellclose Square, we realized that all hell had broken loose: the union lorry had been overturned and police snatch squads were in action. I got separated from my wife and, consumed by fear and worry, we had a row when we found each other agian. We went to the back of the Square, where guest speakers were sitting in the marquee, chatting, while the pitch battle was going on a few yards away. The speeches from the platform continued, but none of them bore any relevance to what was going on in front of the speakers. It was like a bad dream.*

During a brief lull in the police charges, we decided to head for Glamis Road where a residents' march was due to take place, but it had already set off. On our way back to the main gate we saw lorries coming out of Wapping Lane and it was only 9.30pm. We saw BJ and got him away from the place. He had obviously had a drink and was willing to fight the police. The intensity of their attacks on the crowd was far greater than had occurred during the May demonstrations.

Later that night, the demonstration was the main story on national television and radio news and occupied much of the coverage on Sunday. On Monday the Home Secretary, Douglas Hurd, gave a speech in Parliament praising the police action against 'the thugs' and stating that, with the imminent introduction of the Public Order Act, trade unions might have to find another way to demonstrate.

He was joined in his condemnation by Neil Kinnock and Norman Willis, both of whom stated that there was no place in the Labour Movement for those involved in the violence. Kinnock described those who had reacted to the police action at Wapping as 'outcasts'.

Frank: *I wouldn't necessarily approve of violence, it's one of those grey areas. It's still a bone of contention as to who actually initiated the violence on the nights of 3rd May and 24th January. There are those who say it was the demonstrators and there are others who say it was police agents provocateurs. It's all a bit uncertain. I wouldn't champion violence on either side, but I have to admire those people who were at the front when there was trouble. When the decision was made on a Saturday night to push us back off the road to reopen The Highway, very often there were fists flying and I do admire those people who were in the forefront all the time. What annoyed me was that whenever there was violence, when the police charged and there were truncheons flying, there were always people back in Wellclose Square, way behind the 'firing line', shouting at the police, calling them 'vicious bastards'. They were very verbal and very indignant but, in my opinion, if you feel that strongly you should get down there and tell them to their face. I didn't have much respect for those people.*

Joyce: *There was a Women's March at Christmas time. I'd never been on one before and Ann Field came up to me with a candle and a loud-hailer. I looked at the candle and said, 'you are joking. What are we on here?' She said, 'do you want the loud-hailer?' and I said, 'I don't think I'll be in need of it with my voice, do you?' We had a laugh about it.*

I remember talking to Brenda Dean, I introduced myself. I had a can of beer in my hand, I always took one to lubricate the voice. Ann gave Brenda a candle and I said, 'ooh, you'll have to watch yourself Brenda, you'll get done for having an offensive weapon', and she said, 'so will you'.

Anyway, we set off with the candles and were handed a song-sheet and I thought, 'oh good, somebody's changed the words of the carols: there had been some brilliant strike songs over the months. But when I read them they were the real words. Then a girl at the front next to Brenda started singing 'Little Donkey' through the loud-hailer. I couldn't believe it, I thought, 'this is a farce, this isn't really happening, I'm dreaming this'. And I started singing, 'I'd rather be a picket than a scab' ... 'Little Donkey', do me a favour. And I could see all these old ladies looking at me.

But that was the idea, that it should project the usual symbol of women as Earth Mother. But I said, 'what is this, peace and love and make the sandwiches, is this what we're reduced to after all these months? Peace and love and light me a candle sister. Come on'. But I can see that Brenda would think it was a good image: women the peace makers instead of big, macho, pickets beating up Old Bill and chucking smoke bombs.

Denise: *In the end, it became a dispute between us and the police, rather than us and Murdoch. They were seen as strike-breakers. A lot of the time I felt more animosity towards them than I did towards Murdoch. I saw a lot of them, but never saw him. I didn't feel too good about people throwing bricks. At the point where the lorries hit Commercial Road there was always a lot of it going on and I was concerned that it could cause a lorry to swerve and hit someone coming the other way in a car. I can understand people's need to do it though: it was pure frustration. They stood at Wapping all night and the papers were still getting out. They saw nothing being done and finally they resorted to violence. Nobody in the rest of Fleet Street had been asked to come out in support. Nothing had been done about the distribution of the papers. The TUC would not expel the electricians. It was pure frustration.*

Like the case during the Miners' Dispute, where they dropped a slab over a bridge and killed the mini-cab driver. That was terrible, but having gone through our dispute, you can understand how those people were driven to do something like that, whereas before I didn't understand. You think, 'God, that's terrible, how can people do that sort of thing?' Now I can understand.

Graham: *Our rage was justified, these people were carrying out Murdoch's plan. But I remember asking our people who were lobbing bricks if they had thought about what might happen if a lorry swerved out of control. They just said, over and over again, 'yes, but look what they're doing to us'. Most of them would have been horrified if something had happened, but they were blinded by their anger. Some may not have cared. Either way, it was criminal. The tragedy of the mini-cab driver killed during the Miners' Strike was the ultimate consequence of such action, but neither the desperate situation faced by the miners, nor our own agony, warranted such measures.*

Pam: *To be honest, I didn't have a lot of conscience about it, my only real concern was that a lorry might go out of control and go into innocent people.*

But I can't honestly say I cared much about the lorry drivers getting hurt. I stopped thinking of them as human beings. I stopped caring about the horses too. I hated the horses, they were a police animal. I think I learned to hate an awful lot during that time and it's taken a long time to get rid of that nasty feeling. I had a really bad feeling, but maybe that was what kept me going through it all.

There was one time, I think it was when we were trapped in Dock Street. After it had broken up and the horses had gone away, about three of them came back and some kids were throwing stones. I honestly felt that if I had a brick I would have thrown it, I was so angry. I was lucky there was nothing available, I would have done it. I know it's wrong and I would have felt terrible if someone had got hurt and fallen off their horse, but emotions were running very high.

Deidre: *I wasn't a good shot. I swung at a lorry's wing mirror once and was pulled off on a few occasions, but once I discovered I was pregnant I had to stop. But personally, in the situation we were in, peaceful demos were hopeless. It sounds terrible, but I really think we should have done more damage. I think it was war, I really think it was.*

27

The End

On Tuesday 27th January the FOCs/MOCs meeting took place at Caxton House and was attended by Danny Sergeant. When asked where Brenda Dean was, he replied that 'it was not her turn'. Many people were angry that the General Secretary was not present, particularly after the events of the previous Saturday. However, what they did not know was that she was in New York secretly meeting Bill O'Neill, of News International, in an effort to get the company to make an offer which would allow her to end the dispute.

The following week, she sent another written report to the FOCs/MOCs meeting. She said that during the course of the previous week, News International had decided to take action against SOGAT in the Courts. Her report was brief and stated that 'in continuing to organize demonstrations and refusing to discipline our members, we are very vulnerable to sequestration and a further heavy fine'. Her absence at the meeting was due to having met with News International the previous evening. This meeting was attended by Bill O'Neill from News International and Geoffrey Richards from their solicitors, Farrers. Richards had written the memorandum to Murdoch advising him on how to dismiss his workforce without any compensation. Brenda Dean said of Richards, 'actually I got on rather well with him'.

It was at this meeting that the deal was struck. News International agreed to pay the monetary compensation that had already been rejected by the strikers in October and, further, not to proceed with the court action against SOGAT. In return, Brenda Dean agreed that the union would call off the strike without a ballot of the strikers. The meeting also agreed that Farrers would send the union a formal letter, warning of the court action that News International was going to take, which included seeking sequestration and compensation. Armed with the conference decision to keep the union from being sequestrated, Farrer's letter threatening court action and the compensation offer, Brenda Dean prepared her report and recommendations for the National Executive meeting which was due on 5th February.

Since the anniversary demonstration, there had been concerns among the strikers that attempts might be made to end the dispute and, consequently, two officials from each of the striking chapels travelled to the union's headquarters at Hadleigh in order to be present while the executive committee met. Carol and George Hall attended on behalf of the clerical chapels and, at 5pm, Carol rang Caxton House with the news that the strike had been called off.

The Executive had voted by 23 to 9 to end the dispute without a ballot of the members, stating that ballots were for company offers, not NEC decisions. Carol stated that Brenda Dean had blamed the 'militants' who continued to 'take the gate' and the refusal of people to come forward to be disciplined.

With the decision made, the union contacted the company in order for them to carry out their side of the deal and make the compensation offer that had been rejected by the strikers in October. News International then gave the NGA an ultimatum of 24 hours to follow SOGAT in calling off the dispute, or face being taken to court.

Within 24 hours a letter, signed by Brenda Dean, was dispatched to all strikers explaining the NEC decision. The majority of the letter concerned the threat to the union of sequestration and the consequences that this might have on the future of SOGAT and she concluded by saying:

> 'We wish there had been an alternative to the decision which had to be taken. There was not. We could not allow the union back into sequestration. We did not get the industrial support we needed to win, nor was the financial support forthcoming either. Many people have helped us, but they were too few to turn the dispute in our favour'.

The letter made no mention of the failure to win an industrial dispute by using a boycott campaign and, more importantly, it did not thank the strikers for the efforts and sacrifices they had made.

Deidre: *I hadn't taken an active part in the strike for three months because of the baby being born and I heard about the decision on the news. I was feeding her and I burst into tears. I wasn't really surprised, I was disgusted, really disgusted.*

Denise: *I felt so disappointed and angry. I could quite cheerfully have told them to stuff their money. I didn't want the money, I didn't even want it. But there was no way we could have kept going on our own. We all felt so badly let down. We hadn't let ourselves down, we would have done even more if we had*

had better leadership. I felt angry towards the leaders, but you couldn't fault our own people like John, Liz, Carol. It was upsetting to think that everybody had put so much into it and then the National Executive decided they wanted to call it off.

Pam: *When we were shouting about being sold down the river, Brenda Dean said, 'there is no river to sell you down', as if the rug had been pulled out from under our feet and there was nothing we could do. It was only the fact that we were so insistent, through the ballots, that she had to go back in there and put on the pretence of fighting it. But I think she had accepted that it was inevitable, that Murdoch had the law, the system and government backing him up. That's what we were up against.*

Frank: *We all knew. For months and months we'd been saying they were going to sell us out eventually. We knew it was coming, but when it happened we thought, 'what do we do now?' Terrible, terrible.*

It's difficult to try to express your feelings. I wasn't surprised but, at the same time, you did feel a tremendous sense of let down and sorrow that that was the way it had finished after all the effort that so many people had put in. I did nothing compared with lots of people: when you consider that they travelled the country day in and day out. To see it all go, just like that, it really was sad and you thought, 'oh hell, so this is what it's come to, a complete sell-out and over a year of real effort'. It was a great disappointment, but I don't regret one minute of it.

I think our chapel officials did a great job and morale was boosted a hell of a lot by holding weekly meetings. You may have had your doubts, I suppose most people did. You got a bit down and began to think, 'we're not going to win this'. I came to that conclusion after the first month or so. At first I had the optimistic idea that there may have been some kind of truce whereby we'd all go back, with a commitment that talks would take place with a view to a 50% reduction in staff within 12 months, or something like that. But after the first month or so, when it didn't happen, when you saw they were producing the papers and were getting better at it every day, I came to the conclusion that we were not going to win in the sense that we would all go marching back with our banners and all that sort of thing. That became a lot of empty optimism really. But the weekly meetings boosted your morale and certainly strengthened my resolve to go on.

Denise: *I think that any other General Secretary would have been proud of us.*

The joint clerical committee met on the morning after the NEC decision, with Carol and George reporting back on the events at Hadleigh. The information included the fact that, after the Executive had taken its decision, Brenda Dean had given interviews to the television and newspaper reporters present before meeting with the chapel officials. Although there was anger and bitterness about the NEC's decision, there was unanimous acceptance that the dispute had come to an end and arrangements were made for a chapel meeting to take place to recommend this decision to the members.

The SOGAT FOCs and MOCs met in the afternoon. Tony Issacs, from the Machine Branch, opened the meeting by stating that, in his opinion, the 'dispute continues'. The chapel officials reported on their committee's decision that morning and, in an effort to show the futility of the situation, posed questions of the London branch officials about their willingness and ability to carry on with the dispute independently of the national union.

None of the officials present expressed an opinion. It was agreed that the meeting would reconvene on Tuesday 10th February, by which time all the chapels would have had the chance to meet with their members. As the meeting broke up, news came through that the NGA and AUEW National Executives had decided to call off the dispute.

Despite the NEC decision and an instruction in Brenda Dean's letter on the 6th February that 'with the ending of the dispute all demonstrations and picketing should cease forthwith', around 3,000 people turned up at Wapping on the following Saturday evening. There was a huge police presence and a scaffold tower, with cameras and microphones attached, had been erected inside the plant perimeter facing The Highway. In addition, in Virginia Street a large generator was being used to power sets of floodlights.

The police may have been preparing for trouble but, apart from the usual anger and venom expressed towards the scabs entering and leaving the plant, the mood was peaceful. There was a real community spirit among those present and, as well as a feeling of defiance, there was an acceptance of the situation and a realization that this would be the last time so many would gather together outside the plant to protest against the injustices that had occurred.

Two days later, on 9th February, the last full meeting of the TNL/NGN clerical chapels took place at St Brides Institute. The Institute was attached to St Brides Church, which had connections to the printing industry dating back to the late 15th century.

Graham: *I went to my first chapel meetings at St Brides in the early sixties, a 16 year old* Times *messenger desperate for the aged FOC (who was probably only in his forties) to stop droning on so I could escape to some Soho rhythm 'n' blues club. This time there was no such conflict of interest.*

The old place was looking very down at heel, with peeling brown paint doing its best to hide the room's pleasing architectural detail. Old tubular-framed chairs with fraying canvas seats were set in rows and a trestle table and make-shift public address system stood on a rickety platform at one end of the room. It was a far cry from the opulence of the TUC or the University of London, where previous important meetings had been held.

Slowly, in sombre mood, people began to arrive and talked together in subdued tones while the hall filled. More chairs were called for as members crammed in and overflowed into an ante-room at the back. Then, from the platform, Liz Short, flanked by Carol and George Hall and John Lang, called for order.

'This is the most important meeting I have ever chaired' she began, and immediately put the chapel administration's motion that '... the dispute be considered at an end and that the compensation offer be taken up collectively and with dignity'. It seemed shockingly abrupt.

Unusually, nobody wished to speak on the motion. There was an air of resignation, a recognition that the dispute was really over and there was nothing more to say. The vote was taken: 30 for and 3 against. The rest, some two or three hundred people, abstained. 'I know it's over, but I just can't bring myself to vote for it', was the common explanation.

George Hall made his final speech, outlining the shameful events that had occurred at the NEC meeting at Hadleigh, as honest and combative as ever, followed by his wife Carol, her voice quiet and unsteady with emotion. John Lang complimented the members for their commitment, imploring everyone to continue fighting for the same values in their new jobs – and all the while embarrassed at his inability to stem the flow of tears streaming down his face. Then Denis stood up in the body of the hall and asked, simply, for the meeting to thank the chapel officers for their unstinting work throughout the strike. Everyone in the room stood and applauded, releasing a great swell of pent-up emotion so intense, you felt you could touch it. I stood in the middle of it all and felt like my head was going to burst.

I hadn't wanted the strike to end, but I felt a strange emotion when the meeting was finished: a kind of euphoria. I was running around trying to get everyone I knew to go to the pub. I suppose it was relief that it was all over: all the pressures of having no money and worrying about one's family would not disappear overnight, but we wouldn't have to go on coping with people's apathy, or even hostility, towards us. We wouldn't have to do any more picketing and we wouldn't have to face the police again. But, more than a sense of relief, it was an overwhelming feeling of just wanting to be close to everyone who had been involved in the strike. I didn't want them to drift home, I wanted to be with them a bit longer. I felt such empathy and a bond with them all.

I finally left the pub with Dave White and, when we got on the bus, there was the inevitable bloke reading The Sun. *Dave was so upset, I had to stop him snatching the paper out of the bloke's hands and doing something daft.*

Frank: *It was a very emotional meeting and I got the impression that most people regretted that it was over although, understandably, they were breathing a sigh of relief. At the same time, there was a feeling that it should not be the end of people's relationships. It was the end of the dispute, now we had to look around and decide what we were going to do: jobs and the future. But there was a belief that whatever we did as individuals, we must not lose that comradeship that had built up over the year. Most people left with tears in their eyes. It was a very sad night indeed.*

I believe what we did was important and right. The great pity is that, in the end, it didn't achieve anything. We must have thought it was important or we wouldn't have kept on would we? We would have said 'sod this, we're wasting our time' and we would have drifted away. We would have had doubts as to whether we had done the right thing. I have never, for one moment, doubted the rightness of what we did.

28

Hardships and Relationships

Pam: *I'm a widow and I had some money from my husband's pension fund. It was invested for my old age, but I had to use it. I'd lost my job, my own pension and now my husband's money was going as well. I had the anguish of wondering, 'what the hell am I going to do if I don't get a new job soon?' But there was no point in worrying about my old age when I had kids to look after! Karen was at university, Jacquie was still at school and I needed to see John frequently* (Pam's son John was at a school for children with learning difficulties in Wales).

I think something happened to me mentally during the strike. I became a lot stronger and learned to come to terms with things as they are. After my husband died I never quite faced up to things and when the dispute started I was completely floored. I couldn't concentrate like I used to, I couldn't sit down and read a book. I was unsettled. I still am unsettled, and yet I've stopped worrying about my security so much: the less you've got, the less you worry about losing it. It sounds corny, but I've come to the old maxim about taking one day at a time.

Michele: *I felt sorry for the single people because they didn't have anyone to go home to, especially after a gloomy night at Wapping. I was lucky to have a partner who was supportive. We got married during the dispute. I think the marriage was made in The Highway.*

Denise: *I lived on credit and towards the end of the strike I had to start paying it back. I had to pay our mortgage and what I'd borrowed on my credit card. I did some really stupid things like, if you've got two pounds, you'd go out and buy a pound of mince and a packet of spaghetti. But with the card, I was going out and eating a £20 meal. It was silly, but that's what I was doing. I had to pay it all back. I'm still paying it back. But it was an outlet. It's a peculiar thing, I don't know if it's peculiar just to women, but if you went out with a new jumper on, feeling you looked nice, maybe your morale was a bit higher. You'd turn the heating off, then go out and buy something silly. But I never went out on a Saturday night because we were at Wapping and Sunday was spent licking our wounds.*

Tim: *My dad is 78 and my Mum is 67 and it brought it home to me just how old they are and how much things like this affect people. They were*

178

humiliated over something I'd done. I was under pressure from them to get another job, to give up. They said, 'why are you doing all this for the union, they're not doing anything for you. You shouldn't be going off demonstrating, you've got paid officials to do that. You should be looking after your family. The union people are getting paid and they're letting you down. They're going home to a nice house in Berkshire and you're coming home to eviction'.

We spoke to the council and they just said, 'no, you've got to come up with some money'. But there wasn't any money to come up with. I just thought that I must turn to the only people who would help me, the people at the chapel, and I went to see John.

John: *T lived in Greenwich with his elderly parents and when they couldn't meet the rent repayments I wrote to the leader of Greenwich Council on their behalf. I also found out that two of the Greenwich Councillors were members of SOGAT. The Mayor was actually a striker, while the other bloke worked at* The Mirror.

The Mayor sent his fraternal greetings, saying that he hadn't been to Wapping much due to the pressures of his Mayoral duties and, in October, he took the money. It no longer seemed worth pursuing T's case with him, so I put it to the other bloke: 'you're a Labour councillor boycotting the News International titles. Are you willing to let this kind of pressure be put on someone who is fighting for the same principles?' His justification was that the housing officers were not elected, were not Labour officials. I said, 'if you go ahead with this, I'll make sure people find out about it and it will be very embarrassing for you'. I think that was what did the trick.

Pam: *Jacquie, my younger daughter, would say to me, 'I would have gone in', or, 'why don't you just go and get another job, it's the obvious thing to do. You can't live without money'. She wasn't interested at that age. But I could always approach a serious topic with Karen, my older daughter. Maybe, because I got angry with her and started explaining things in more detail, she began to understand. She began challenging her friends at university who bought* The Sun. *She worked in the local newsagent's shop on Saturdays and she would get quite bolshie with people if they came in and asked for it. 'Are you sure?' she would say, 'wouldn't you be better off with* The Mirror?'

My cousin's daughter and her husband were both police sergeants and I was hearing, through them telling my mother, that I should keep away from Wapping, that things were going to get worse down there. Another time they said I shouldn't keep going because, if I did, I would never get a job. I think they must have meant the surveillance cameras. I went down once for a meal with them and we talked, very carefully, around it. I gathered that they didn't like going there. They didn't like what was going on and, in fact, his younger

179

sister and her husband, who were also police (it ran in the family) actually left the force because of Wapping. I don't know whether it was the violence, or political, but they got out pretty quickly.

Mick: *I had some very good friends who didn't really get involved in the dispute and when it was over they said, 'well, you got your money anyway'. But that wasn't the point and I can't get on with them now. I suppose the strike was an awakening for me and they just haven't woken up yet. We're not on the same wavelength and my attitudes to everything are different now. I don't have friends who didn't sympathize with the dispute. Nobody I know buys Murdoch's papers. I wouldn't talk to them if they did.*

Tim: *They say, 'you forget about it now. You've got your money, you've done your year's penance, so don't go on about that Socialist crap. Just go back to being a normal boy. And don't you stick up for nobody else, you've got your money, just forget about it'.*

John: *It's like GP and his nan and grandad. They were still getting the papers during the dispute, so he asked them to stop buying them. They said 'no' and he said he wouldn't visit them until they did. They'd had a very good relationship. He went round again and asked them if they'd stopped and they said 'no' again. They couldn't understand. He broke up the family. His mum asked him to go and see them but he wouldn't. He said, 'I hate my nan and grandad. They don't understand what they're doing to me'.*

My mum told me I'd lost my sense of humour, but I thought my sense of humour was what kept me going through the dispute. But I'm not as flippant as I used to be, I think things are a bit more serious. My mum and dad supported me all the way through and the best thing that happened to me was when they came down to Wapping. My dad was annoying me, saying he didn't think they'd go. But my mum knew I was upset and she made him.

When we got there, she saw the police and she saw how angry people were, standing at the fence shouting. She said she'd never seen such anger before and she got really angry herself. Then she got talking and everybody was saying, 'oh, you're John's mum'. She talked for three hours without knowing who anybody was and she said she hadn't seen that kind of spirit since the War. It was like the old East End, she said. I know it's a bit of a myth, but she said people used to talk to each other during the War. They only had each other, so they used to talk a lot. People don't bother to talk any more. She thought it was brilliant and I think that night did more to make her understand the strike than anything I said to her during the whole year. If only we could have got everyone's parents, brothers and sisters and friends down there. It's not the same on the telly. You still feel safe indoors!

Marie: *I got married to Manuel during the strike – something which raised my spirits and also cheered up a lot of people. Some were having a hard time, relationships were busting up and some were losing their homes. Our wedding meant a day out for about 30 of the strikers and an opportunity to celebrate something Murdoch couldn't touch.*

Graham: *The dispute dominated our lives. It haunted us wherever we went and whoever we were with. Everything else seemed insignificant. Rightly or wrongly, the everyday things our friends outside the strike did appeared trivial beside the harsh realities of Saturday nights at Wapping and living on Supplementary Benefit and when, inevitably, we got around to talking about the dispute, they couldn't comprehend our depth of feeling.*

But the strike had become, for better or worse, the greater part of us. Even those who sympathized with our stand could not be expected to display the same sort of commitment we did and if someone was actually hostile to the cause, it became very difficult to keep a friendship alive. The ground had shifted. It was no longer enough to have run together in the same school playground; to have grown up in the same street; to have shared good times and bad, because we felt it too deeply to be able to accept their dissension and go on as if nothing had changed.

Before, friendships had survived differences of opinion over even important issues, but this was different because we were actually living and breathing every bitter moment of it. For their part, it was an unwanted intrusion and they couldn't understand that it mattered so much to us, that it was important enough to threaten a long-standing relationship. But for us, nothing mattered more.

Family and friends could be unbelievably insensitive. They would leave a copy of the Sunday Times *in an armchair. They couldn't understand why you wanted them to stop taking* The Sun: *'but we only get if for the bingo'. Some even managed to go through a whole year, a year replete with television pictures from Wapping showing bleeding print workers and their wives, without mentioning the strike once. Not once! And when you suggested that, perhaps, they might like to support you by wearing a 'Don't Buy The Sun' badge, or putting a sticker in their car window, they just giggled. And if they did respond to events at Wapping, it was to accuse you of being irresponsible for taking your wife.*

The argument that one should not have subjected one's wife and family to such hardship was common. A typically narrow, conservative point of view which puts family considerations before everything and everyone else, never mind one's responsibilities to the broader family of community, or workmates. In other words, look after number one.

I don't believe the strike made any real impression on my own very young children, although my wife suffered a great deal. She says it was the worst year of her life. At The Times, I had a relatively well-paid job by clerical standards and it was good, for once, not to have to worry too much about paying the bills. But, during the strike, money was tight and Cathy worried about the mortgage repayments and eked out the supplementary benefit buying food and the kids' clothes. She hated having to count out the pennies in the local shops and sometimes she just could not bring herself to go. But in the depths of despair, eight months into the dispute, at the time of the second ballot on redundancy money, I asked her (despite knowing what her answer would be) what she would do if she were voting instead of me. Without hesitation she said, 'I'd vote No'. Her answer came out of a fundamental morality and a deep sense of injustice at being forced into poverty.

Now, a year after the end of the strike, tears still well up in her eyes every time the dispute is mentioned. She fights to hold onto cherished friendships undermined by it and puts to the back of her mind the knowledge that the people closest to her let her down. She carries a mixture of sadness, resentment and anger, typified in something she repeats whenever she is forced, for it is always against her will, to talk about the strike. 'Murdoch has so much to answer for. Surely, one day, he will have to pay'. She paid a high price for sticking to her guns. Everybody did.

I explained to friends what had happened on 3rd May: that the police were not deployed to keep public order, but used politically, to ensure that Murdoch got his papers onto the streets and the unions were broken. They argued that the police had merely done their duty. They conceded that a few 'bad apples' may have misbehaved, but inferred that we got what we deserved because we put ourselves into a compromising position by taking part in the marches, a position that they would never have put themselves in. I said the police acted under orders, that the violence was orchestrated. In that case, they argued, they were bound to obey those orders without question. I said 'what about personal integrity and responsibility?' They said that we should not demand, or expect, the highest standards from the police, that they are only human and that we had to accept that they were, and always had been, used for political purposes. We were living in different worlds.

'Was it worth it?' I hear you ask. 'How foolish and naïve to try to stand in the way of progress'. But this 'progress' was nothing more than one man's ruthless pursuit of power. You either accept being manipulated and live in the shadow of capitulation, or you say, 'that's wrong, I won't accept it'. If we had been sacrificed so that new technology could produce independent, principled newspapers, you might have a point.

John: *The chapel had always encouraged those closest to the strikers to attend the weekly meetings, the idea being to prevent families from feeling isolated and for people to have an opportunity to share problems and experiences. The meeting on 14ᵗʰ March was held at the TUC headquarters at Congress House and was fairly vociferous, with arguments between branch officials and members of the chapel.*

At the end of the meeting, the regular strike payments were made and, as people climbed the long flight of stairs to the street, one of the children, Sarah Johnson, was separated from her mother, Rosie, and fell through a gap under the handrail on to the stone floor below. She died that afternoon in hospital.

I made the following entry in my diary:

One of the saddest days I've ever known. Griff's daughter fell from the stairs at the TUC where we were holding our meeting. She died later in hospital. I was on my way to Leeds to speak at a meeting when I heard. Everyone absolutely stunned. Cried. Everything that happened at the meeting, including my own ranting and raving, seems totally insignificant now.

For me personally, and I know for many others, Sarah's death was one of the main reasons that drove me to resist anything that Murdoch, the Government, the police and even our own union could throw at us.

The print unions in London rallied round Rosemary and Graham 'Griff' Johnson and a stained glass window memorial for Sarah was installed at SOGAT's rest centre at Rottingdean. It's impossible to describe the grief and suffering they endured and it's testament to their courage, and their belief in the strike, that they rejoined the picket line at Wapping.

Afterword

- In 1991, the NGA and SOGAT merged to form the Graphical, Paper and Media Union (GPMU). The membership elected Tony Dubbins as General Secretary and Brenda Dean as his deputy.

- Dean resigned her post in May 1992 and, in July 1993, became Baroness Dean of Thornton-le-Fylde, taking her seat in the House of Lords.

- In 2002, the GPMU merged with the engineering union Amicus which, in 2009, became part of the general union Unite.

- The EETPU was expelled from the TUC in 1988 for refusing to end the negotiation of no-strike deals with employers. In 1992 it merged with the Amalgamated Engineering Union (AEU) to form the Amalgamated Engineering and Electrical Union (AEEU), a move which saw the electricians readmitted to the TUC.

- In 2001, the AEEU was absorbed into Amicus which, as previously stated, became part of Unite in 2009.

- Prior to the 1986 dispute, there were approximately 40,000 print union members in London. Today there are around 4,000.

- The anti-union laws of the 1980s are still in place, despite the fact that a Labour government has held power for 13 of those years.

- The Police Complaints Board Authority and the Crown Prosecution Service carried out an investigation into police behaviour at Wapping during the anniversary demonstration on the 24/1/87. Despite some 440 complaints against more than 100 officers, no police officers were prosecuted.

- In December 1993, Wyn Jones was sacked from his post as Metropolitan Police Assistant Commissioner for alleged misconduct.

That month, responding to a question in the House of Commons, the then Home Secretary, Michael Howard, stated:

> '... Following a review ... of the evidence relating to Mr. Wyn Jones's conduct, the then Commissioner of Police of the Metropolis informed my predecessor in October 1992 that he regarded Mr. Wyn Jonses's behaviour as reprehensible and wholly inconsistent with what was expected of someone holding the office of Assistant Commissioner.'

In 1995, Mr. Wyn Jones was convicted of stealing food and wine worth £24 from Marks and Spencer.

● News International withdrew recognition of the National Union of Journalists at Wapping in 1989, and has not recognised unions at any of its four national newspapers since. Instead, the News International Staff Association (NISA) was set up to represent all staff at the four titles. NISA is funded by the company and has been refused recognition as an independent trade union. The Certification Officer for Trade Unions decided that NISA could not establish that 'it was not under the domination or control of an employer' and 'not liable to interference by an employer'.

● The four titles are no longer printed at Wapping and Kinning Park. In 2008, around 600 jobs were lost when production was moved to new plants at Broxbourne in Hertfordshire, Knowsley near Liverpool, and Glasgow.

● Keith Winfield, a member of the TNL clerical chapel during the strike, died on 7th December 1987. He was 28 years old and had failed to find work since the dispute ended. Fearing he might never work again, Keith threw himself from the window of his flat.

Sources

Chapter 1
Interview with clerical striker, 1987

Chapter 2
Harold Evans, *Good Times, Bad Times* (Weidenfield and Nicolson, 1983)
Michael Leapman, *Barefaced Cheek* (Hodder and Stoughton, 1983)
William Shawcross, *Murdoch* (Chatto and Windus, 1992)
Article entitled 'Foot demands debate on future of The Times' by Ian
    Aitken, *The Guardian*, 23 January 1981
Article entitled 'Blood and thunder at Printing House Square' by
    Laurence Marks, *The Observer*, 25 January 1981
Article entitled 'Times deal cost £12 million' by Stephen Cook, *The
    Guardian*, 14 February 1981
James Moran, *NATSOPA, Seventy-Five Years, A History of the National Society
    of Operative Printers and Assistants* (University Press, Oxford, 1964)

Chapter 3
Len Murray, speech at special Trades Union Congress Conference
    held at Wembley, 4 April 1982
Bill Keys, *The Guardian*, 21 January 1983
Mark Dickinson, *To Break a Union, The Messenger, the State and the NGA*
    (Booklist Ltd, 1984)

Chapter 4
Article entitled 'Murdoch evening paper "a sham"' by Patrick
    Wintour, *The Guardian*, 8 January 1986
Article entitled 'Mr Murdoch's bouquet of barbed wire' by Patrick
    Wintour, *The Guardian*, 22 January 1986
Article entitled 'Print workers battle for future' by Patrick Wintour,
    The Guardian, 25 January 1986
Linda Melvern, *The End of The Street*, (Methuen, 1986).
Socialist Worker, September 1985
London Post (Printers) Limited initial proposal re London Post to
    SOGAT Clerical Branch

Quote from Frank Chapple re Eric Hammond, *The Guardian*, 29 January 1986

Eric Hammond, *Maverick: The Life of a Union Rebel* (Weidenfield & Nicolson, 1992)

Letter from Geoffrey Richards of Farrer & Co. published by *The Morning Star*, 21 February 1986

Chapter 5

London Sogat Post, February 1986. Report of the mass meeting held at Brixton on 13/1/86

Interview with Rupert Murdoch, *The Sunday Times*, 19 January 1986

Linda Melvern, *The End of the Street* (Methuen, 1986)

Interviews with clerical strikers, 1987

Chapter 6

Letter to staff of Times Newspapers Limited, signed by Bill O'Neill, Director.

Interviews with clerical strikers, 1987

Author's Diary, 1986

Chapter 7

Interviews with clerical strikers, 1987

Article entitled 'Behind the Barbed Wire' by Peter Wilby, *New Socialist*, March 1986

Chapter 8

Interviews with clerical strikers, 1987

Chapter 9

Interviews with clerical strikers, 1987

Chapter 10

London Strategic Policy Unit Briefing Paper, *Policing Wapping: An Account of the Dispute 1986/7*

Quote from Tony Dubbins, General Secretary of the NGA re picketing, *The Guardian*, 28 January 1986

Article entitled 'Picket line lesson for local school', *The Wapping Post*, 18 May 1986

Article entitled 'Lining up for a spot of Wapping overtime', *The Wapping Post*, 25 October 1986

Chapter 11
Interviews with clerical strikers, 1987

Chapter 12
Interviews with clerical strikers, 1987
Carmel Bedford and Jean Sargeant, *A Sign of the Times: The Women in the Wapping Dispute*

Chapter 13
National Council for Civil Liberties, *No Way in Wapping,* April 1986
Author's Diary, 1986

Chapter 14
Brenda Dean, *Hot Mettle, SOGAT, Murdoch and Me,* (Politico's 2007)
Author's Diary, 1986
Interview with clerical striker, 1987

Chapter 15
Interviews with clerical strikers and clerical striker's wife, 1987

Chapter 16
Letter from Brenda Dean to all members of News International, dated May 1986, giving details of the National Executive Committee's decision to seek release from the Order of Sequestration.
Letter (undated) from Chris Robbins on behalf of the London District Council to all members of News International giving details of press release and intention to hold a mass meeting.
Letter from Chris Robbins on behalf of the London District Council to all members involved in the News International dispute, dated 19 May 1986, proposing escalation of the dispute and distributed to strikers as they entered the mass meeting held on 19 May 1986.
Letter from Brenda Dean to all members of News International, dated May 1986, giving details of talks that had taken place with the company, the offer they had made, and a ballot form to vote on that offer.
Press release from London Machine Branch, dated 29 May 1986, giving details of legal challenge regarding the distribution of ballot forms.
Letter from Charlie Cherrill, Branch Secretary of the London Machine Branch, to all members in dispute with News

International, dated 29 May 1986, giving details of supplementary points that had allegedly been agreed with the company.

Letter from Brenda Dean to all members of News International, dated 30 May 1986, giving details of supplementary points and stating that these were not being voted upon in the ballot.

Interview with clerical strikers, 1987

Author's Diary, 1986

Chapter 17

Report of the Biennial Delegate Meeting of SOGAT, June 1986

Article entitled 'The power to defeat apartheid' by Neil Kinnock, *The Sunday Times*, 20 July 1986

Letter from Brenda Dean to all branch secretaries, officers and organisers, dated 1 August 1986, giving details of Order issued by the High Court.

Article entitled 'Depot recovering after ugly attack', *The Thetford Times*, 2 August 1986

Letter from Danny Sergeant, General President of SOGAT, (unspecified to whom), dated 6 August 1986, giving instructions on how picketing and demonstrations should be conducted.

Interview with clerical strikers, 1987

Author's Diary, 1986

Chapter 18

Article entitled 'Hammond gave Wapping go-ahead' by Patrick Wintour, *The Guardian*, 20 November 1986

Letter from Brenda Dean, General Secretary of SOGAT, with ballot form attached, dated September 1986.

Interview with clerical striker, 1987

Author's Diary, 1986

Chapter 19

Interviews with clerical strikers, 1987

Chapter 20

James Moran, *NATSOPA, Seventy-Five Years* (University Press, Oxford), 1964

Interviews with clerical strikers, 1987

Author's Diary, 1986

Chapter 21
Letter from Rupert Murdoch to all News International strikers, dated 31 October 1986.
Letter from Brenda Dean to all News International strikers dated 31 October 1986.
Letter from Rupert Murdoch to 'all dismissed News International employees' (undated)
Interview with clerical strikers, 1987.
Author's Diary, 1986

Chapter 22
Article entitled 'Willis believed sacked printers must compromise' by Patrick Wintour, *The Guardian*, 8 November 1986
SOGAT Journal, November 1986
Interview with clerical striker, 1987
Author's Diary 1986

Chapter 23
Article entitled 'Prisoners of Wapping', *The Wapping Post*, 15 November 1986
Brenda Dean, *Hot Mettle, SOGAT, Murdoch and Me*, (Politico's 2007)
Interview with clerical striker, 1987

Chapter 24
Interview with clerical striker, 1987

Chapter 25
Article entitled 'Mine Fuhrer', *The Sun*, 15 May 1984
Interview with clerical striker, 1987
Author's Diary, 1986 and 1987

Chapter 26
Interview with clerical strikers, 1987

Chapter 27
Brenda Dean, *Hot Mettle, SOGAT, Murdoch and Me* (Politico's 2007)
Brenda Dean, report to News International FOCs, dated 2 February 1987

Letter from Brenda Dean to all members of News International, dated 6 February 1987, giving gives details of decision to call off the strike.
Interviews with clerical strikers, 1987

Chapter 28
Interviews with clerical strikers, 1987

Afterword
Article entitled 'Wapping verdicts', Leader comment, *The Guardian*, 25 January 1990
Article entitled 'Former Met chief on theft charge' by Heather Mills, *The Independent*, 4 October 1994
Article entiled 'Celebrity setbacks that have stolen the limelight' by Sally Pook, *The Daily Telegraph*, 15 December 2001
Hansard, 16 December, 1993
Article entitled 'NI staff association denied recognition as trade union' by Jean Morgan, *Press Gazette*, 25 May 2001
Article entitled 'Murdoch's revolutionary £350m presses' by Stephen Brook, guardian.co.uk, 17 March 2008

More stickers from 1986